Short and Sweet

STORIES FOR PREACHERS AND TEACHERS

by
Frank Barron

THE COLUMBA PRESS
1991

First edition, 1991, published by
THE COLUMBA PRESS
93 The Rise, Mount Merrion, Blackrock, Co Dublin

Cover by Bill Bolger
Origination by The Columba Press
Printed by
Biddles Ltd, Guildford

ISBN 1 85607 030 1

Copyright © 1991 Frank Barron

Contents

	Thematic Index	5
	Introduction	7
1.	Run it through her again	9
2.	A sup of brandy might help	10
3.	All in all, quite a get-up	11
4.	Billy the Knocker	12
5.	Mind my boat	13
6.	How would you catch a monkey?	14
7.	Not on my bus, they didn't!	15
8.	The cat and dog story	16
9.	My little red hen	17
10.	A Mercedes or roller skates	19
11.	Suffering	20
12.	My friend Jerry	21
13.	Throw me the fish	22
14.	Just trust me	23
15.	Together we can do anything	24
16.	Faith must be lived	25
17.	Heaven on earth	26
18.	Try to get it straight	27
19.	Hospitality	28
20.	Moaners seldom give	29
21.	You can go on your own	30
22.	Splinter in your own eye	31
23.	It depends on how you look at them	32
24.	To praise is to please God	33
25.	Search for the truth	34
26.	The butcher's boy	35
27.	Drop the price-tag	36
28.	An optimist or a pessimist	37
29.	Good buy in an Irish monastery	38
30.	Mind that poor donkey	39
31.	Show me the way	40

32.	No help is too small to give	41
33.	Dad, my turtle is dead	42
34.	Would you like a preview?	43
35.	It's a small price for love	44
36.	You must go into partnership	45
37.	He will lift you up	46
38.	Hide and seek	47
39.	The greatest gift	48
40.	I will light a candle to guide you	49
41.	I appreciate that friend	50
42.	They say one good turn deserves another	51
43.	We must send the furniture ahead of us	52
44.	I love you that much	53
45.	Drawing wrong conclusions	54
46.	Maybe you are part of the problem	55
47.	Junk or treasure	56
48.	I can hear a cricket somewhere	57
49.	Stop struggling and I can help you	58
50.	The local shopkeepers	59
51.	Always give your best	60
52.	A new way of seeing	61
53.	I witnessed a miracle	63
54.	Kindliness	64
55.	Don't miss your chance	65
56.	Please God, help mam to start the car	66
57.	Let him touch you	67
58.	How do you really feel?	68
59.	Poor Marilda	69
60.	Keep your eyes on the ball	70
61.	Love can change anything	71
62.	Cool it! Have patience!	72
63.	The answer is at the centre	73
64.	He does answer, you know	74
65.	You must turn the latch	75
66.	Blessed Virgin Mary	76
67.	Just reach out and touch him	77
68.	Gossip	78

69.	Don't run away – face it	79
70.	Give it your best shot	80
71.	Bad language	81
72.	Message of peace	82
73.	It isn't the Church – it's you	83
74.	No excuse Sunday	84
75.	Ten most wanted individuals	85
76.	The world is mine	86
77.	Everyone is lovable	87
78.	Finish the story for me, please…	88
79.	Crocodiles are seldom friendly	89

SOME PROP HOMILIES

80.	God is here	91
81.	Unique and useful	92
82.	The power of words	93
83.	The black spot	94
84.	The mirror and the pane of glass	95

Thematic Index

The numbers refer to story numbers and not to page numbers.

B.V.M. 55, 66, 67.
Church 16, 50, 72, 73, 74, 75.
Commitment (Marriage) 8, 10, 11, 61, 63, 70, 72, 77, 83.
Conversion 1, 7, 20, 52, 70.
Conscience 30, 45, 63, 70, 75.
Co-operation 2, 9, 15, 23, 50, 51, 72.
Death 40, 46.
Encouragement 21, 24, 54, 58, 62, 79, 81.
Faith 5, 14, 16, 25, 36, 37, 38, 48, 52, 60, 69, 78, 80.
Forgiveness 35, 46, 53, 62, 83.
Gifts (Talents) 2, 15, 51, 71, 81.
God 12, 25, 31, 37, 38, 55, 80.

God's love 1, 22, 44, 49, 56, 57, 60, 61, 63, 64, 66, 67.
God's mercy 1, 10, 49, 53, 57, 62, 83.
Happiness 3, 8, 17, 28, 59, 61.
Heaven 31, 34, 40, 43, 51.
Honesty 13, 18, 71, 75.
Jesus 11, 14, 29, 36, 55, 61, 63, 65, 67.
Judging 3, 16, 20, 22, 26, 30, 36, 45, 68, 82, 83.
Kindness 2, 42, 54, 57, 62, 67, 83.
Loneliness 49, 58, 65.
Love for others 17, 19, 23, 27, 29, 32, 34, 39, 43, 51, 58, 59, 61, 62, 75, 77, 81, 83.
Materialism 6, 13, 18, 33, 46, 50, 51, 52, 55, 65, 74, 84.
Praise 24, 59, 61, 82.
Prayer 4, 21, 49, 56, 57, 60, 64, 70, 74.
Prejudice 7, 45, 46, 59, 72.
Saints 3, 12, 19, 29, 32, 38, 75.
Searching for God 31, 47, 48, 52, 55, 56, 63, 65.
Selfishness 6, 27, 29, 33, 34, 39, 51, 55.
Sharing 15, 19, 58, 59, 61, 62, 81.
Suffering 11, 49, 52, 58, 60, 69.
Thanks to God 41, 56, 57, 74, 76.
Trust in God 5, 12, 14, 36, 49, 50, 52, 53, 57, 60, 61, 64, 65, 66, 67, 69.
Truth 7, 10, 13, 16, 22, 25, 29, 48, 60, 69, 82.
Work 9, 43, 51, 55, 70, 72, 81.

Introduction

Every good mother knows what it is to sit at the bedside of her child, often till she is pale in the face, and begin her next bedtime story with, 'Once upon a time …' That love of story leaves a stamp on all of our lives. When it comes to storytelling we are all children. Jesus, the great teacher, used stories to get across most of his most powerful messages.

A story has a great ability to reach all of us where we are at. I have often used a story in preaching to bring across a specific message, and, after the service or Mass, someone would come in to thank me for sharing the message with them – but the message they got from the story was completely different from the message I had in mind! So, although I have drawn up a Thematic Index for reference purposes, please use the stories as they touch you.

In today's world, many are very quick to switch off if the Gospel message threatens their lifestyle in any way. The implications might often be, 'How dare God tell me how to live my life!' Storytelling is a great tool for reaching the inner conscience of a materialistic age. There is one powerful example in the Old Testament, where the Prophet Nathan would not dare to approach the king directly to tell him that he was wrong. The king would simply have him killed, and then continue to live as always. But if you read chapter twelve of the Book of Kings, you will see how Nathan forced the king to examine his conscience by the use of a story. I believe that we are inclined to remember and reflect on a story, long after we would remember even the bones of a straightforward sermon.

Most of the stories in this book I had originally written into a shabby brown notebook many years ago. I have forgotten where many of them came from or what made me write them down. I never really thought they were good enough for publication until many friends and fellow-priests pushed me into putting them together as a book. [If you don't like the book, you can blame them!]

I have always enjoyed preaching, throughout my priesthood, and I still feel humbled by the fact that many hundreds of holier and more talented people than I am, sit in church feeling obliged to listen to my feeble efforts. I remember one night, after one of the first missions I ever gave, I was walking up and down beside the church with a fellow-missioner. An old lady approached me and said, 'I am very deaf, father, and I can't hear your lovely, humble sermons.' To save myself embarrassment, I said very loudly in her ear, 'Ah, mam, you are not missing much.' 'So they're telling me,' she replied.

One night, my fellow-missioner was preaching on marriage and, again walking together outside the church, we overheard some of the people coming out and talking about the mission. One of three ladies asked the others, 'What did you think of that?' 'Ah, sure, isn't he the grand little fellow?' replied the second. The third member of the group gave a dirty little laugh and added, 'Yes, but I wish I knew as little about marriage as he does!'

Communicating God's message is not easy, and all of us can only do our best. I hope that you find these stories of some help on a Saturday evening preparing for a vigil Mass, or when you're trying to find a story to kick off with, or even when you're preparing a class in catechetics.

Frank Barron

1. Run it through her again

A few years ago I was talking to a Wexford farmer and he told me of an incident that happened some time earlier. I am suspicious, as I am sure you will be, that there is a slight exaggeration. It goes like this: A young twelve-year-old youth from the local town came looking for some summer work and the local farmer took him on a week's trial. The first job he gave him to do was to go out and milk one of the cows by hand. So the young lad went off with the bucket and the farmer told him to join him in the house for a cup of tea when he had finished. Twenty minutes passed and there was still no sign of the young lad with the bucket of milk. Twenty five minutes passed, but when the half hour was up the farmer was getting impatient and he leaped up from the table and out to the cow house to see what was happening. He screamed with rage when he saw what was happening before his eyes. 'Young Tommy,' he shouted, 'what are you doing giving the bucket of milk back to the cow?' At this stage, the youngster was shaking with fear and he answered, 'Sir, Sir, she put her leg in the bucket and dirtied the milk and I am running it through her again!'

I doubt if that young lad made a success as his methods do not work in farming, but they do with the Lord. In the scriptures this is what Jesus asks us to do. He reminds us that no matter what our sin has been, no matter how we have made a mess of life, we should come back to him and believe that he will give us a fresh start.

2. A sup of brandy might help

Did you hear about the good Christian family who wanted to do everything possible for their 85-year-old mother who had grown very sick? The doctor suggested that they should give her a small glass of brandy each night to help her digestion. However, she was a very religious woman and she refused to take it. They then offered her a glass of milk which she graciously accepted. So, religiously, each night they would get a fine big glass, fill it three quarters full of milk and then fill it to the brim with brandy. For two years she drank the mixture, licking her lips not to miss the last drop. Then came the end, when she was called to God's eternal peace. From her death bed she spoke to her family and her final words were: 'By the way, never sell that cow!'

Such a family would be richly rewarded by God, because each simple thing they did was to give comfort, joy, happiness and love to their mother. We also are called to love, each day that we live. We may all dream of showing love in some dramatic way and of doing something exceptional to show God how much we love him. But for most of us, we are asked to show the love of God to others in the ordinary simple things of life: our time to those who are lonely, our hands to those who need our help, our forgiveness to those who need our forgiveness, our love to those we find it hard to love, our friendship to all men.

I heard once a recipe for happiness and it went something like this:
  Take five ounces of patience,
  a pinch of hope,
  then take two handfuls of industry,
  a packet of prudence,
  a few sprays of sympathy,
  a bowl of humility,
  a jarful of spirit-of-humour.
  Season all this with strong common sense
  and simmer gently in a pan
  of daily content.
Why not try it?

3. All in all, quite a get-up

Some years ago, I was walking up a street in Enniscorthy when I noticed a strange looking character walking up in front of me. He wore long yellow hair, plaited on one side of his head and a closely chopped blue colour on the other side. He had Texan-type boots and trousers that looked like pyjamas - all in all, quite a get-up. There was an old blind lady standing at the top of the street trying unsuccessfully to cross through the traffic. She heard him approach her, so she called out to him, 'Oh please, would you help me to cross the street?' I waited for his reaction. Frankly, I expected him to just grunt and walk on ... but no ... 'Of course I will,' he said and he gently took her by the arm and helped her across the street. Having reached the far corner of the street she thanked him saying, 'I am so grateful to you as I was afraid to cross on my own.'

He walked back again and I met him at the top of the street and, for conversation, I said to him, 'That is your good deed for the day.' Firstly he just grunted and began to walk away, but then he stopped and walked back to me with a sense of joy on his face and said to me, 'You know, padre, I feel good. I feel really good because I have done something for somebody today. Sadly, if the gang was with me I would not have had the courage.'

Would you have the courage to be different? As you and I end each day, do we have reason to be joyful because we have done something for somebody?

There is a second point: If the lady had good sight and could see this strange looking character coming towards her, would she have asked him for help? My guess is no, she would have pre-judged him as a 'no good' and let him pass by. Don't we often pre-judge people by first appearances, presume them to be good, bad or indifferent.

We must open our hearts in love to all people, and invite them to share our love, and let the risen Christ be their judge.

4. Billy the Knocker

Illustration: You could use a little box as a visual aid.
You may have heard about Billy. He was very well known and liked in his small community. A religious man also, he went to Mass each day of his adult life. However, Billy always had a pain some place – in his head or his ear or his nose or his hand or his elbow or some place. Almost every morning after Mass, he would go down to the doctor's house and knock, looking for a tablet for something. So much so that the local people named him 'Billy the Knocker'. Billy died, and secretly, although he could not dare say it, the doctor was glad – he had enough hardship from him.

A month later, the poor doctor himself got a heart attack and died. His coffin was put down next to Billy's to rest in peace. But the first night he heard a knock on his coffin which he ignored. But then the knock got louder and louder. In the end he answered, 'Yes! Who is it?' 'Oh doctor, it is Billy. Have you any cure for worms?'

Without prayer we cannot hope to experience peace with God. Prayer is our life-line to God and, without it, we become a very empty people. If we could imagine a little box ... we do not realise how empty it is until we take off the lid. In similar ways, we often do not see the need for prayer, or the value of prayer, until we face struggle or tension or worry or suffering in our lives. In such circumstances, if our prayer life is active, we will feel an inner strength, we will feel the touch of God.

5. Mind my boat

Some years ago, I went to visit my sister who lives in Thomastown, Co Kilkenny. It was one of my nephews' birthday, so I brought him into town to buy him a present. There was a toy boat in one of the shop windows and this really caught his eye. In we went and purchased this little timber boat with a long string attached. On our way back home as we passed over the River Nore, he begged me to let him leave his boat out into the water. It was a cold, damp evening with a thick fog down that made it impossible even to see the far side of the river. However, since it was his birthday, I decided to give in and he let his boat out into the river. After a few minutes, I said to him, 'Pat, maybe some big fish has gone away with your boat.' He just shook his head and continued to walk up and down the bank. A few minutes later I said to him, 'How can you be sure that something has not gone off with your boat?' 'Well,' he said, 'I can't see it with the fog, but I can feel something tugging at the end of my string.'

In our search for God in life, we would love to have concrete evidence. We would love to have something dramatic happen to us that we could be certain of God's presence. In times of doubt, in times of suffering and stress, we would love to have some definite proof that God is working in our lives. However, most of us will not be privileged to experience miraculous powers or healing, but if our hearts are open, we will feel the presence of Jesus tugging in our hearts.

Before the first Easter Sunday, many people were full of doubt. They had seen Jesus die a terrible death on Good Friday. But, then came Easter Sunday morning and news began to spread that Jesus was risen. The authorities had spread the rumour that the body of Jesus had been stolen, so the people were very confused and uncertain. But, as time passed, the people became sure beyond all doubt that Jesus had really risen. And the reason the people were sure is the same reason that my nephew knew his boat was not stolen:

they felt the tug of Jesus in their lives,
they felt the power of Jesus at work in their hearts.
May we open our hearts to feel his presence in our lives.

6. How would you catch a monkey?

Illustration: A jar big enough to get your hand into.
Forgive me now if I try to teach you how to catch a monkey, as they used to catch them in the jungles of Africa.

The African hunters used to get a jar like this, and tie it to some heavy object. They would then put a nut or some hard food, that the monkey would love, into the jar. The idea is that the adult monkey's paw would just fit into the jar to catch the food. But then, with the food in his paw, he would be unable to pull it out. Of course, he could release the food and go free, but he won't, because the monkey is selfish. And so the hunter catches the monkey because he gets trapped by his own greed.

'Stupid monkey!' we may say, but remember we Christians do the very same thing. We may not get caught in a jam jar, but so often we are not free to love fully because we become trapped in greed or money or power or work or materialism or apathy. Unless our hearts are open in real love, we will only show half love, half concern.

7. Not on my bus, they didn't!

A tourist operator hired a bus to bring a group of people around Ireland. The bus driver was obviously very nationalist-minded, and, in every town that they passed through, he would say something like, 'Now this is the place where the Irish beat the stockings off the English!' As they visited areas like the Boyne, he would say, 'This is where the Irish ran the English home in 1641.' As he would pass through Enniscorthy, he would say, 'This is the place where the Irish ran the English off Vinegar Hill in 1798.' He would refer to 1594 and 1848 and many other dates, but in all cases the Irish would have won. About the third day, after about twenty different examples of occasions when the Irish were supposed to have beaten the English, a very mannerly Englishman came up to the bus driver and asked, 'Sir, did the English win any war during all their time in Ireland?' The bus driver turned around, looked him straight in the eye, and said, 'Not on my bus they didn't!'

We all accept that this is not a true account of what actually happened. We relate it in jest. However, when we look at all the prejudices that we meet in life, they are equally ridiculous and exaggerated. We could take examples from politics, religion, business life, social life, between neighbours, and, saddest of all, occasions when prejudice tears family life asunder.

8. The cat and dog story

The old couple had just returned home from a function to celebrate their fifty years of marriage. They put on a big fire and relaxed in front of it. The room was warm and cosy. Even the cat and dog were in front of the fire enjoying the heat it gave. After some time, the cat and dog began to play with each other. Tears were coming from Maggie's eyes as she watched them. Eventually she said, 'Jack, look at them. Isn't it lovely to see how well they get on together?' Jack took his eyes from the paper, lowered his glasses a bit, and said, 'That's OK, Maggie, but you tie them together and you will see what will happen!'

If you tie a cat and dog together, what was once a cosy friendship would probably become a battle ground. But when two people are joined together in the sacrament of marriage, that seed of love should continue to grow and grow. It is a happy day if a man can get up at his Golden Jubilee dinner and genuinely say, 'It seems like only yesterday.' But it is sad if he feels like saying, 'And if it was tomorrow I would cancel it.'

9. My little red hen

Once upon a time, there was a little red hen who scratched about the farmyard until she uncovered some grains of wheat. This hen had been brought up to be a good provider and a good community-conscious hen. She called her neighbours and said, 'Times may be bad, so let's do something for ourselves. If we plant this wheat we shall have bread to eat. Who wants to be involved in this project? Who will help me to plant it?'
'Not I,' said the cow.
'Not on your life.' said the duck.
'Not I,' said the pig.
'No chance,' said the goose.
'Then I will do it,' said the industrious hen, and she did it.

The wheat grew tall and ripened.
'Who will help to reap the wheat?' asked the little red hen.
'Ah, it's not my thing.' said the duck.
'Out of my classification.' said the pig.
'I'd lose seniority,' said the cow.
'I'd lose my unemployment benefit,' said the goose.
'Then I will,' said the hen, and she did.

At last the time came to bake the bread.
'Who will help me bake the bread?' asked the hen.
'That would be overtime for me,' said the cow.
'I'd lose my supplementary benefit,' said the duck.
'I am too tired,' said the goose.
'Then I will,' said the little red hen.

She baked five loaves and held them up for all the neighbours to see. They all demanded their share. 'No!' said the hen, 'If you did not work for it, you don't deserve it.'
'Excess profit,' yelled the cow.
'You capitalist!' cried the duck.
'I demand equal rights!' shouted the goose.

The pig just grunted and walked off in a sulk. Then they planted 'Unfair' signs and marched about with their hands in their pockets all day.

Then the government officials came and reminded the little red hen of the regulations (rule 999), which stated that you can earn as much as you like, but the authorities can take most of it from you and give it to those who don't care. The little hen's neighbours wondered why she never again baked bread.

Here is the problem:
Where do we fit into the story?

10. A Mercedes or Roller Skates

One afternoon, three men arrived at the gates of heaven and all three were interviewed in turn by St Peter. He spoke to the first man and asked him, 'How often were you unfaithful to your wife?' 'I am sure I was not as good as I should have been but I tried,' he said. St Peter answered him by saying, 'You were a very good Christian and I am going to reward you well for a good life. You may go into heaven and you can have a Mercedes for all eternity.' St Peter turned to the second fellow and asked him the same question. But he spoke up confidently and said, 'St Peter, I have lived a very good life and I was always very good to the wife and family.' 'Now,' answered St Peter, 'You seem to have a very short memory. What about the times you got drunk and left the family short? Nevertheless, otherwise you were not so bad. You may go into heaven and you may have a Morris Minor for eternity.' The third fellow tried to bluff his way. It had often worked down on earth, so he tried it with St Peter. He learned very quickly, however, that this is the one occasion when you cannot bluff. St Peter reminded him of all the selfish things he did on earth. He was sent into heaven and given a bicycle.

About three weeks later, on a spilling wet day, the fellow on the bicycle stopped at a red light and, there beside him, was the fellow in the Mercedes, crying. He banged at the window and said to him, 'It is I that should be crying out in all this rain.' 'Ah,' he answered from inside the car, 'It is not like that at all. I have just seen my wife going down the other way on Roller Skates.'

In this life there are so many contradictions. The good seem to suffer and the evil seem to go free. The selfish chancer may seem to win when the honest Christian will be hurt. Scripture reminds us, however, that in the next life each one of us will be rewarded according to the quality of our lives.

11. Suffering

A Chinese peasant lived in a small village with his wife and teenage son. Through much hard work, he was able to buy a mare. 'You are so fortunate to have such a fine mare,' said the villagers. 'I am only human, and only the Gods know of good fortune,' replied the old man. One day the mare ran away. 'How unfortunate,' said the villagers. 'I accept the judgement of the Gods,' said the man. Some days later, the mare returned, followed by a fine stallion. 'Now you have two fine horses. You are indeed a lucky man!' cried the townspeople. 'I know that only the Gods know,' said the old man.

The old man's son decided that he would break the stallion so that it would be able to help with the work on the farm; he was thrown off and broke his leg in six places, making him limp very badly. 'Alas, now your beloved son is lame for life,' said the villagers. 'Only the Gods know why,' said the old man. Weeks passed, and a company of soldiers came to the village and took away all the young men to fight in the army - all but the lame young man. The villagers gathered at the old man's house to congratulate him on his good fortune at being able to keep his son. 'You were right,' they said. 'Only the Gods do know.'

We could continue this story with numerous other examples, but they would continue to make the same point, namely, that it is difficult to judge whether many happenings in our life are for good or bad. We can all reflect back on life to incidents that seemed to be bad but turned out for good. We also realise that, if all of us received all that we dream of, we would not find happiness.

Never lose hope. Turn to the Lord.

12. My friend Jerry

As a young lad, growing up in Gusserane in Co Wexford, I used to hear a story about a kind old man of the road. He was constantly seen with a big bag on his back. Nobody knew what was in the old bag and nobody ever asked. One day one of the neighbours offered Jerry a lift on his horse and cart. He got up on the back of the spring car and off they went. After a while, the neighbour turned round to say something, and he noticed that Jerry still had this heavy bag on his shoulders. The neighbour suggested that he leave down the bag on the car and give himself a rest, to which the old man replied, 'Ah sir, you are good enough to carry me. You do not have to carry my bag as well.'

We often approach God in the same way. We go to God in prayer but do not fully trust him. We do not place all our worries, our needs and our suffering in his hands. We continue to keep our hearts closed. Like Jerry, we continue to keep our burdens on our backs instead of handing them over to God.

In St Matthew's gospel (11:25), Jesus says 'Come to me all you who labour and are overburdened and I will give you rest. Shoulder my yoke and learn from me, for I am gentle and humble in heart and you will find rest for your souls.'

Just as a young child will fear no danger provided Mammy has a tight hold of its hand, in the same way let us hold the hand of the Lord as we face the worries of life, the situations of life that we are afraid of.

13. Throw me the fish

This man was a bit of a fishing fanatic, and what made it even worse was that he never caught many fish. The wife used to give him hell, reminding him of all the work that he should be doing about the house. Sometimes she would really rub salt in the wounds when she would say, 'I wouldn't mind if you were any use at fishing.' This day, Paddy was coming home after one of his fishing outings and as usual he had caught nothing. He decided to go to the fish market to buy a few fish. He asked the woman behind the counter how much were the fish. 'Twenty pence a fish,' she said. He handed her a pound note and walked about six feet away and said to her, 'Ah mam, would you throw me five fish?' 'Might I ask you,' she said, 'why am I to throw them at you? Can't you take them off the counter yourself?' 'No, no,' he answered, 'You see, I want to tell the wife that I caught them and you know I never tell her a lie.'

That silly story might be a parable for a much more serious side of life today. Areas of our Christian life, like honesty, seem to some to be out of date. We may have less people stealing £20 from their neighbours' pocket, but there are thousands of slicker, more professional forms of dishonesty that are equally bad and unChristian, but we pretend not to see.

14. Just trust me

One of my favourite stories in the gospel is the beginning of chapter five in St Luke. It is very easy to picture the scene on that day. For many years Peter, James and John had made their living fishing on the lake of Gennesaret. This morning, they had just come back in, having fished all night and caught absolutely nothing. They were bending over their nets, repairing them where necessary, to be ready for the next evening's work. Jesus came walking along the beach, followed by a great number of people, all anxious to hear him speak. He asked Peter if he could use his boat as a floating pulpit and, of course, he was glad to assist Jesus.

When Jesus finished speaking that morning, he made a request that was a bit hard to take, and I will tell you why. Peter knew all that there was to know about fishing in those Gennesaret waters. He knew, from all his experience, that it was ridiculous to let down the nets in the daytime when the great heat of the sun would drive the fish into the cool depths, far out of the reach of any of the nets. They had just finished a long spell of work on the sea all night and, besides this, they were very tired. Now they were being asked to do something that would make him appear very foolish in the eyes of other fishermen. I imagine part of Peter felt like telling Jesus to get a bit of sense and to keep preaching and to leave the fishing to him and his friends.

In spite of all this, Peter's reply was a model of obedience to and trust in the Lord. 'Master we have laboured all night and caught nothing, but, if you say so, I will let down the nets.'

In these simple words we have the perfect example of Christian obedience and absolute trust. Each day we may be challenged to open our hearts to the inner voice of God.

15. Together we can do anything

I have a brother, Jim, who lives in the United States for the last twenty five years. He served some time in the Vietnam War and, in the midst of the misery of that war, gained many good friends. In his home one night in Albany, New York, I met one of his friends who told me of an incident that happened to him in Vietnam. A group of them were out patrolling a small post when they were ambushed and a few bombs dropped in the middle of them. They ran to save their lives into the woods. After running frantically for about a hundred yards, he fell and realised that he could see nothing. He lay down quietly hoping not to be seen and did not move for what seemed like hours. After a long time, he heard groaning and he realised that someone was dragging himself towards him. It was his comrade who had broken his leg and was not able to stand up, but he could see him in the distance and had come over as soon as it seemed safe. One could not see where to go, and the other could see but was not able to walk. Eamon picked his friend up in his arms, and was guided by him as they walked along. After six hours of walking, they got back to the main camp, both realising that they could not have made it on their own.

As he told his story, I realised that what they did was the secret to all life – alone we can achieve very little but together we can achieve anything.

16. Faith must be lived

A priest and a soapmaker went for a walk together. The soapmaker said, 'What good is religion? Look at all the trouble and misery of the world after thousands of years of teaching about goodness, truth, and peace - after all the prayers, sermons and teachings. If religion is good and true, why should this be?' The priest said nothing. They continued walking until he noticed a child playing in the gutter. Then the priest said, 'Look at that child. You say that soap makes people clean, but see the dirt on that youngster. What good is soap? With all the soap in the world, the child is still filthy. I wonder how effective soap is after all.' The soapmaker protested and said, 'But, Father, soap can't do any good unless it is used.' 'Exactly,' replied the priest. 'So it is with our religion or any other religion. It is ineffective unless it is applied and used.'

So do not blame religion for the problems of the world, blame rather those who reject it or those who wear the tag of religion but do not live by it.

17. Heaven on earth

In 1980 my brother came home from America with his family. His daughter, Yvette was four years old at that stage and she stayed at our family farm in Gusserane, Co Wexford, for three months that summer. She had the time of her life and obviously enjoyed every moment of her time about the farm. She was spoiled sick by her grandparents and got anything she asked for. One day she was walking down through one of the fields with her grandad and she asked him a question that left him startled for a bit. 'Grandad, will heaven be as nice as Gusserane?'

How grateful we should be for anyone and everything that makes a 'heaven on earth' for us, and the best way that we can show our gratitude is to make a heaven for anyone we can. The following anonymous lines were sent to me some time ago, and they might give us some idea of the ideals that we must aim at.

A little more kindness, a little less creed,
A little more giving, a little less greed,
A little more smile, a little less frown,
A little less kicking a man when he's down,
A little more 'we' and a little less 'I',
A little more laugh, and a little less cry,
A little more flowers on the pathway of life,
And fewer on graves at the end of the strife.

18. Try to get it straight

A conversation overheard between a grocer and his son went something like this:
'Have you fixed the scales so that we can cut the weight on all the items?'
'Yes, Dad.'
'Did you mix the white sand with the sugar yet?'
'Yes, Dad.'
'Did you put the grade A sign on all that cheap coffee that we bought the other day?'
'Yes, Dad.'
'Good, son! Hurry up then to bed – and make sure to say your prayers!'
'Yes, Dad.'

We may smile jokingly at the contradiction in this conversation but its attitude may be much more a reality than we care to admit.
In society today we accept contradictions as a matter of course. How sad!
We have come to presume that there is corruption in so many businesses and we just count ourselves lucky if we are not caught. How sad!
We are not the slightest bit surprised to hear of corruption in politics. We are, in fact, pleasantly surprised to find things otherwise. How sad!
Honesty, uprightness, fairness, respect - such virtues seem to be associated with the unenlightened of our business world. How sad!
In the last thirty years, we have achieved so much, in the material sense, but at a very big price.

19. Hospitality

The children in a local school were preparing for their Christmas Pageant. The teacher wanted them to act out the Christmas Story. Little Paddy, from fourth class, was asked to act the innkeeper, even though he did not like being the bad fellow who would not let Jesus in. Every time Paddy practised his part he almost cried, he felt so bad, even though the teacher explained that he was only playing a part.

When it came to the day of the performance, Mary and Joseph crossed the stage to the door of the inn. Paddy answered the knock. There was a sob in his voice when he said, 'No Room.'

Then his true feelings came to the surface. He opened his arms and, in a high voice said, 'Come on in anyhow, and have a cup of tea.'

Kris Kristofferson had a song called 'The Taker'. He reminds us that we are all either givers or takers. Each one of us must ask which we are.

20. Moaners seldom give

A few years ago I was at a function and one of my little nephews happened to be with me. Before the function started, we sat on a table inside the door of the hall with about six other people. We chatted about all the vitally urgent matters of life, like the weather and 'Do you come here often?' and 'What's the food like?' and 'How well we know the hotel owners?' As the people started to come in, one lady took over and she gave us a running commentary on the breed and activities and looks of everyone who came in, including a few things my eight-year-old nephew could have done without. As we went home afterwards, I intended to find out in a roundabout way how the little lad reacted to all of this. But just as we came out the door, he said 'Uncle Frankie, wouldn't that auld one give you a pain in your face? Did you hear the things she said about all the nice people that came in. I wouldn't mind,' he said, 'but I wouldn't want to put her face up in a frame in my bedroom either.'

I imagine if all of us could hear a tape of all that we say about people, we might be very embarrassed: The bad word about people instead of the good word, the criticism instead of the praise, the suspicious comment instead of the trusting one, the judgemental comment instead of the merciful one, the hateful word instead of the loving one.

So much depends on the way we look at life. But one thing is certain, if you want to find happiness within yourself, you will find it by loving and lose it by knocking. And did you ever notice that moaners seldom give, and givers seldom moan? Above all, remember if you haven't given, you haven't loved.

21. You can go on your own

Last summer, I met an old school pal who has been working and living in London for many years. The day I met him, he had his twelve-year-old son with him and, on one occasion when the son had left the room, Pat told me of an incident that happened about six months earlier. Every day that the son was not at school, he would go with his Dad to work. He must have travelled on the same subway, and got on and off at the same stops, hundreds of times, but yet he was afraid to go anywhere on his own. This concerned Pat, so, at noon one day at the office, he said to his son, 'Tom, I want you to go home now and help your Mom. I will take you to the subway.' Young Tom was full of fear. Tears were coming in his eyes as his father waved goodbye to him at the station. What Tom did not realise, however, was that his Dad slipped into the next carriage and was with him all the way back. But Tom never relaxed, frightened as he checked the name of every station. Only when he got out on the platform, one street from his home, did his face begin to relax. It was then that his Dad caught him by the shoulder and smiled. 'Oh Dad,' said Tom, 'I would not have been the slightest bit frightened if I had realised that you were there.'

As we walk our journey through life, we are often so frightened and afraid. We so often try to work out all our problems, but we are unsure and there may be times when we are confused and do not know where to look for an answer. There may be times when we are hurt and we do not know how to find healing. Times when we are angry and we do not want it to fester, but we feel we have not the strength to rid it from our lives on our own. It is on such occasions, when we feel unable to cope with life's problems, that we must firmly believe the scriptures, which constantly tell us that Christ is always with us to strengthen us, to heal us, to support us and to love us. 'I will be with you all days,' Jesus promised, 'until the end of time.'

Try to realise and experience how close God is to you tonight.

22. Splinter in your own eye

A man once stole some food and was ordered by the king to be hanged. When asked if he had any last words, the thief replied, 'Know, O king, that I can plant an apple seed in the ground and it will grow and bear fruit overnight. It is a secret that my father taught me and I thought it would be a pity if it died with me.'

A time was appointed the following day for planting the seed. The thief dug a hole and said, 'This seed can only be planted by someone who has never stolen or taken anything which did not belong to him. Being a thief, I cannot, of course, do it.'

The king asked his prime minister to plant the seed. But he hesitated and said, 'Your majesty, when I was young I recall keeping an article that did not belong to me. I cannot plant the seed.'

The treasurer, when told to plant the seed, begged the king's pardon saying that he may have cheated someone out of some money. The king, in his turn, recalled that once he took and kept a precious object belonging to his father.

Then the thief turned to them and said, 'You are all mighty and powerful persons. You are not in want of anything, yet you cannot plant the seed. Yet I, who stole a little food to stay alive, am to be hanged.' The king, pleased with the man's wisdom, pardoned him.

We must be very careful not to pass judgement on anyone until we have first looked closely at ourselves. The scripture reminds us to take the splinter out of our own eye first so that we will be able to see clearly enough to take the splinter out of our brother's eye.

23. It depends how you look at them

A newcomer arrived into the village of Littletown and he was very curious to know what the villagers were like. The day he arrived he made it his business to get into conversation with one of the old-timers. He asked him, 'What are the people like in this place?' 'What were they like in the place that you came from?' queried the old-timer. 'Well,' he answered, 'They were rotten, mean, lying, dishonourable and selfish, so I just had to get out. That's why I came here.' 'Then,' replied the wise old-timer, 'You had better get out of here, because that is exactly the kind of people that you will find here!'

A few weeks later, another newcomer arrived in the same village and also wanted to know what the people were like. He also spoke to the same old-timer and again asked, 'What are the people like in this village?' Once again the old-timer replied by asking, 'What were they like in the village you came from?'
'Oh, they were lovely, kind, understanding, considerate, friendly and decent. I'm sorry that circumstances forced me to leave.' 'Then,' came the reply, 'You will find the very same kind of people here.'

It all depends on our viewpoint. If we want to see bad in people, we can. If we want to see good, it's there, if only we look long enough.

24. To praise is to please God

A priest went to visit one of the homes in his parish one afternoon. The housewife was very uneasy as she had very little to offer him in the line of food. The day before, she had made a pie but it had not turned out very well. After talking about the weather and other pressing subjects, she offered him a cup of tea, half hoping he would not take it. However, she was not that lucky. He said he would love a cup and also, he said, 'Please give me a slice of that pie that I can see on the counter.' Her blood started to go cold as she saw him eat it and her pride was also hurt since, in general, she considered herself to be a good cook. As he was about to leave, the clergyman praised the pie into the heavens and mentioned that he had even taken a second slice.

Some weeks later, the same priest was coming out to the same family for dinner. This time the housewife made certain that her pie was superlative. The priest ate it without a comment. After dinner, when she got him aside, she had to ask him what was wrong with her pie. 'You praised my pie the other day,' she said, 'And you did not mention my pie this evening, even though it is much nicer.' The priest nodded and said, 'The truth is that the other needed praising.'

We can be slow to give praise and support to one another.
We can be so quick with the criticism and so slow with the affirmation.
We can be so quick to knock and so slow to lift up.

25. Search for the truth

A little lad from Wexford seemed to be acting very strangely after his first day at school. Some time after he had been sent to bed, his mother went up to check on him and she found him staring under his bed. He asked her to stay quiet as soon as she came into the room, and insisted she leave him alone for some time. She came back about one hour later and he was still staring at the ground. At this stage he said, 'Today in school the teacher said that before we were born we were dust, and that after we die we will be dust. This evening I noticed all the dust under the bed, so there must be a fellow in there and I am trying to figure out whether he is coming or going.'

If all of us searched for God with the same enthusiasm and determination as a child for his dreams, there is no doubt that we would feel his presence in our lives.

26. The butcher's boy

A certain butcher delivered meat to the local Archbishop's house every Friday evening. The young apprentice in the butcher's shop hated the job every week, since he dreaded ever meeting the Archbishop. This Friday evening as usual, he rang the door of the Archbishop's house presuming that old Margaret would meet him. However, the Archbishop just happened to be coming out of the house and when the young lad saw him he got such a fright that he almost threw the meat at the Archbishop, said, 'There's the meat,' and took to his heels. 'Wait,' said the Archbishop, 'That is not the way you address a bishop. I will show you. You go inside the house and act an Archbishop and I will take the meat and act the butcher's boy.' So, he rang the door and the young lad opened from the inside. Then the Archbishop, acting the boy, said, 'Good morning, Archbishop. I have meat for you that has been sent up from the butcher's shop, and I hope you have a very enjoyable weekend.' 'God bless you, young man,' said the young lad, and then taking a pound note out of his pocket, gave it to the Archbishop and said, 'Here is a pound for yourself.'

There are always two sides to a story and, before we condemn or even criticise someone, we should put ourselves in their shoes.

27. Drop the price-tag

Tommy was eight, so this oft-repeated story goes. One day, having done several odd jobs for his mother, he presented her with a bill which read:
   For weeding the garden: ten pence
   For going to the shop twice: twenty pence
   For not leaving the soap in the bath: twenty pence
   Total: Fifty pence.

His mother read it and smiled. Expectantly, Tommy waited. But no fifty pence was forthcoming. That evening, as Tommy was going to bed, his mother gave him an envelope in which there was a bright, new fifty pence piece, wrapped up in a piece of paper on which something was written in his mother's handwriting.

Tommy spelled it out very carefully and read as follows:
   For bringing Tommy into the world: nothing
   For taking care of him for eight years: nothing
   For paying his doctor's bills, buying his clothes and
      feeding him all this time: nothing
   Total: nothing.

Tommy looked at his mother and then at the fifty pence piece. There was a struggle going on in the child's mind, but at last he handed the fifty pence piece back to his mother with these words: 'Mammy, I suppose I owe you more than you owe me, so in future I'm going to do things for you like you do them for me – for nothing.'

On a more sophisticated level, do we have a price-tag on our love? Do we say, 'I love you,' but in the back of our mind have many 'ifs'? Remember Christ gave himself freely in love. So must we.

28. An Optimist or a Pessimist

There is a story told about twin boys, one an optimist and one a pessimist. Their father was very worried and he was telling a rich friend, who owned a big department store and a farm, about how totally different they were. One was always happy with everything. No matter how bad it was, he seemed always able to find some good side to it. The other, no matter how good things were, always seemed to find something to complain about. So the friend suggested, 'Well, I'll make a bet with you that we will be able to do something that the pessimistic boy will have to be happy with, and the optimistic boy will have to complain about.'

They took the complaining pessimistic boy to the toy department of the friend's store and said, 'Now you play with any toy you want to in this store and then, when you are finished, pick the toy you like best and you can take it home with you to keep.'

They took the other boy out to the farm and put him in the hot, smelly barn, filled with stinking horse manure and heavy with flies. They said, 'Now we are going to leave you here all by yourself and we will come back in three hours to let you out.'

When they went back to the department store, the pessimistic boy was sitting in the middle of the room crying. He said, 'There are so many toys I don't know which one to play with or which one to bring home.' The father said, 'See, that's the pessimist for you.'

After three hours, they went back to the farm. When they opened the door, the boy was happily shovelling away and cleaning out the barn. 'How could you find anything to be happy about in this stinking, filthy place?' asked his friend. The boy answered with joy on his face, 'Why not? Where there's horse manure there's got to be a pony someplace.'

Happiness does not depend on what we have or own or possess.
Happiness is something we feel inside.

29. Good buy in an Irish Monastery

A group of people went to an Irish monastery to do a weekend retreat. When the retreat was over, at about four o'clock on Sunday evening, and before they set out to return home, they thanked the monks for the nice weekend, for the opportunity to renew themselves spiritually, and for the privilege of attending Mass each day.

As they were driving out of the monastery grounds, they saw a very old woman lying in the ditch. She looked dirty, with torn clothes. She appeared barely alive. As they drove by her, one of them suggested that they should stop and try to help the old woman. They were about to do this, when one lady said, 'Maybe we shouldn't stop. We haven't enough time and I have to play bridge at 7.00 p.m.' One of the men agreed and said, 'Perhaps it would be dangerous to stop. After all, that is a stranger and why should we stop?' So they drove off.

We do not know if the story is true, but whether it is or not, it makes a very important point. Christ lives in every person, the rich and the poor, the healthy and the sick, in the person we dislike, in the person we criticised yesterday, in the person we ignore every day - even in the person we think unlikeable.

30. Mind that poor donkey

A father and his son set off to the local market with their donkey. At the beginning of the journey, the man sat on the beast and the boy walked. Before very long, the people along the way began to complain. 'Look! What a terrible thing! A big strong man sitting on the donkey while the poor little boy has to walk!' So the father decided to dismount and the son took his place. But in a short time the onlookers remarked, 'How terrible! The poor old man walking and that young strapping lazy boy sitting!' At that, they both sat on the donkey's back, only to hear others say, 'How cruel can you get. Do you see those lazy clowns sitting on that little donkey?' So off both of them got and walked. Other bystanders then commented, 'We've seen it all now! Those two fools must have bought a donkey just to look at him. Why don't they get up on the old donkey? That's what he is there for.' Finally, they both carried the donkey but they never got to the market.

Those who say we are a nation of knockers have a lot of truth in what they say. If you want to be popular do very little, don't get involved and be hail-fellow-well-met. Be in the right place at the right time and smile at the right people. That style will probably keep the majority of people happy, but it is not the way Christ wants us to be. Christ himself was the very opposite. He criticised the pharisees for their hypocrisy.

He whipped the money changers out of the temple. He cured the sick on the Sabbath even though he knew he was leaving himself open to criticism.

Christ calls us to follow his example, to do what we believe to be right, even if it means accepting criticism. To say what we believe to be right even if we have to accept opposition. But remember:
You may fool the hopeless public.
You may be a subtle fraud.
You may hide your little meaners,
but you can't fool God.

31. Show me the way

Bishop Fulton Sheen, I am told, was responsible for the following anecdote, told concerning his first visit to a certain city.

Coming out of the station, he stopped a small boy and asked him the way to City Hall. The boy offered to walk with him and show him the way. As they walked along, the youngster commenced to question the then Father Sheen.
'What's your name?'
'Father Sheen.'
'And what are you going to the City Hall for?'
'I'm going to talk to a lot of people there.'
'Well, what are you going to talk about?'
'Oh, I'm going to tell them how to get to heaven.'
'G'wan,' was the reply, 'Why, you don't even know the way to City Hall.'

In life we spend so much time trying to answer all the questions of this life and often avoid the basic purpose of life. Why are we here? Where do we hope to go at the end of life? What can be the purpose of life if there is not something beyond?

32. No help is too small to give

Years ago, after a magnificent cathedral had been built, a gentleman stood outside admiring it. Standing beside him was a little girl about six or seven years old.
'Mister,' queried the little one, 'do you like that church?'
'Yes, my dear, I think it is quite lovely.'
'Well, Mister, I'm glad you like it because I helped to build it.'
'You? You helped to build it?' was the astonished enquiry.
The child nodded.
'But,' went on the gentleman, 'you are only a little girl. How did you help to build it?'
'My daddy is a bricklayer,' came the reply, 'and he worked on the church ever since it began, and every single day I brought him his lunch.'

There is a danger that we will all dream at some stage in life of doing something great for God. But let us serve God in the little things of life and we will experience his peace.

33. Dad, my turtle is dead

I heard a cute story once of this boy who had a pet turtle. Every evening, as soon as he came home from school, he would go out on the front lawn and play with his turtle, who seemed to give the child more joy in life than anything else.

One day, the boy went to the front yard and found the turtle on its back. He went up to check it and there wasn't a stir. He came in screaming, 'My turtle is dead, my turtle has died, what can I do without him?' His dad caught him in his arms and started to promise him all sorts of things to see if he would stop screaming. He promised to make a coffin, to dig a grave, and even to have a little ceremony for the funeral. Then his mom took over as the screams lessened. She promised to have a party after the funeral and he could ask all his friends and she would bake him his favourite cake. At this stage, after all the promises, the tears were replaced with a big smile.

He and his dad walked out to the yard to collect the turtle. But just as they were about to pick it up, it slowly turned over and began to walk away. Both of them stood in amazement for a moment and then little Johnnie shouted, 'Kill him, daddy! kill him!'

We can do the same in life in a less obvious sense. The greatest gift that all of us have received is the Christian message. If we live by the message, we will experience a peace that none of us can buy. We also live in a world of false promises. Any time we put on the TV, we are bombarded with ads which tell us in a very persuasive manner that if we buy A, B or C we will be much happier. There is a great danger that we, like the little child, will throw away what is precious for false promises. Jesus reminds us, 'He who saves life will lose it and he who loses his life for my sake and for the sake of the Gospel will save it.'

How is your turtle getting on? Do you still want him?

34. Would you like a preview?

I heard a story of a man who was well in with St Peter. He asked him to give him just a little look at heaven and hell while he was still here on earth. St Peter agreed and said, 'Tonight, while you are asleep, I will bring you up.'

When he arrived, it was 11 a.m. heaven time, and he went for a look at hell. It consisted of an extremely big room full of big tables of beautiful food, but everyone looked so sad. When he went in to see heaven, it looked the very same, big room, lovely tables with beautiful food, but everyone looked so happy. The man went to St Peter to ask what made the difference. 'Come back at meal-time,' St Peter said, 'and see for yourself.' And yes, here was the secret. Each person had to eat with a five-foot-long chop stick. In hell, they would pick up the lovely food, but could not get it to their mouths and so they went hungry and were bitter and frustrated. In heaven, however, they would pick up the food and feed the person opposite and the person opposite would feed them. Thus, by sharing, they found happiness and peace.

The message for us does not need great explanation. In all of our lives there are two forces at work. One force calling us to reach out to others in love, because Christ loves them and would want us to love them also. But there is a second force, selfishness, that pushes us to think only of ourselves.

The call of Christianity is to make sure that the force of goodness wins in our lives; to make sure we love, even if we feel like ignoring; to make sure that we try to forgive, even if we have hated for years; to make sure that we try to be patient and understanding, even if we feel like screaming; to visit someone who is sick, even when we know we will never be appreciated; to constantly challenge ourselves and ask, 'What would Jesus like me to do tomorrow?' even if I feel like lying about doing nothing.

35. It's a small price for love

I remember conducting a mission in a certain part of the country about seven years ago. While I was there, I was asked to say a community Mass in one of the homes and of course I was privileged to do so. When I came to the sign of peace at Mass, I put on some soft music and asked all thirty people in the room to speak to everyone. After four minutes or so, having noticed nothing strange, I continued Mass. Next morning, one of the men came to see me and said, 'I could have hit you last night, Father, but now I want to thank you. For twelve and a half years I have not spoken to my neighbour next door because of a difference we had over children fighting. During all that time, I used to try to avoid talking to him or meeting him on the road or in the local shop or at the football matches. I even changed my local pub to avoid him. When I went to church, I used to make sure I was not near him in case the priest would have the sign of peace. Last night was no exception. I sat on the opposite side of the room for Mass and, at the sign of peace, I kept one eye on him to avoid him. But at one stage when I turned around he was there and I was forced to put out my hand. When I did so, I got a warm hand-shake back. When I went outside the door he was waiting and he said, 'Thanks, Jack.' Last night, we went to both pubs and maybe I had one too many but for once it was worth it. He thought I had stopped talking to him first and I thought he had stopped talking to me. Both of us realised that it had been so stupid, and now it was like a weight lifted off our shoulders.'

Maybe, as you sit and listen, you could do the same thing. Life is too short to do anything but love. It is definitely too short to tear your heart assunder with hate.

36. You must go into partnership

There is a story told about a young hard-working farmer who one day was looking over his gate into a field. He had just drained a bog and transformed it into this beautiful green field. The parish priest happened to be walking down the road and he walked over to the gate to speak to Paddy, the industrious farmer. The priest casting his eyes across the field said, 'Isn't it great, Paddy, what God can do?' Paddy, obviously a bit peeved that God should be getting all the credit, said, 'Maybe so, father, but he did a damn bad job on it before I went into partnership with him.'

It is God's will that we should use our talents to develop the world in which we live. But it would be very sad if, in the midst of our work and achievements, we should ever forget that God is the author of all life. Sir James Simson, the discoverer of chloroform, was once asked by an interviewer, 'What do you consider was your greatest discovery?' The questioner expected that Sir James would say chloroform, but, instead, the great scientist replied, 'My greatest discovery was when I learned and was convinced that Jesus Christ was my saviour.'

Our prayer should be that, in the midst of the rush and bustle of life, we also will discover a personal relationship with Christ our Saviour.

37. He will lift you up

One summer about ten years ago, my brother Jim was at home on a visit from the States. My three-year-old nephew became very close to him during the four weeks of his visit. During the days before Jim went away again, they were trying to explain to the little lad that his uncle was going back to America on a big plane. The day Jim left, I was at home and, during the day, a plane happened to fly overhead. The little lad came screaming over to me and said, 'Is that my uncle Jim going back home?' I took the easiest way out and said, 'Yes, he is in the big plane.' Then there was silence for a few minutes. I could see the little lad look at the ground, and then at the sky, and back to the ground again. Eventually, he came over to me and asked, 'Uncle Frank, how did my uncle Jim get up into that plane?' I tried to explain to him that the man who drove the plane was so good that he came down to the ground to pick up his uncle Jim, and he would bring him off wherever he wanted to go.

As I was trying to give this simple explanation to a three-year-old child, I began to realise that this is exactly what Christ does for all of us. Christ has promised us that he is close to us always and that, if we turn to him with trust, he will raise us up above all worry all hurt, all suffering, all disappointment. Jesus tells us, throughout the scriptures, that he will raise us up to a peace that he alone can give.

38. Hide and seek

A young boy was preparing to receive the Sacrament of Confirmation. It is a time when many good and committed teachers spend a lot of time and energy challenging the young people to be adult leaders within the Church and society at large.

Stirred by this enthusiasm one young twelve-year-old, called Paul, had a dream the night before his confirmation, not about the amount of money he was going to receive, but about God. He dreamt that God woke him up in the middle of the night and asked him to play hide and go seek with him ... I am sure you played it as a child.

Paul decided to hide first, and for three hours God searched for him in every corner of the house with no success until, in the end, God noticed him. Then it was God's turn to hide. Paul searched for him for five minutes but then he got fed up and went to bed. Half an hour later, God woke him up again and, looking very sad, he said, 'Paul, you were not very fair. I looked for you for three hours but you stopped looking for me after a few minutes.'

Isn't that precisely the relationship many of us have with God? God has given us so much and shown us so much love, as the whole Easter Liturgy makes us aware. God stretches out arms of love and invites us to share a peace that he alone can give. My peace I leave with you, my peace I give you, not the kind of peace the world offers but my peace. But we can so easily ignore his call through boredom, apathy and indifference.

39. The greatest gift

'A bell isn't a bell until you ring it,
a song isn't a song until you sing it
and love isn't love until you give it away.'
The greatest gift that you can give to any person is your genuine love. No money or wealth can buy it.

Just before Christmas I went in to visit in a private nursing home. One old lady had just opened three gifts she had received that day and laid them on a table just beside her bed; an expensive clock, a lovely nightgown, and a silver tray.

I complimented her on her presents. Immediately, I knew I had said the wrong thing, because she burst into tears. 'Oh no, father,' she said, 'these three presents are from my three daughters, who have more money than they will ever need. I don't need their presents but I desperately need their love, their concern and to know that they actually care about me.'

Friends, it is so easy to give things. We can so easily ease our conscience by giving things to people that we know we should thank. The majority of people, however, who are in hospital, living alone or lonely because of any circumstances do not need things from us – they need us. They need our time, our love, our friendship. They need to feel that they are important to us.

In the heavy snow one January, Enniscorthy, where I lived at the time, was almost snow-bound. Everybody was on foot and nobody seemed to care. There was a great bond of love and friendship in the community. Everyone seemed to be conscious of the old and sick and did not want to see them go short of anything. One old lady said to me, 'I hope the snow lasts for a month. I have never seen so many people or received so much real love.' Why wait on the snow to show our love?

40. I will light a candle to guide you

In the 1930's, a middle-aged man lived with his mother in the inner city, Dublin. He worked on the docks and each night his mother would light a candle and leave it in the window to guide him down the back street into his house. She had done this for years and, suddenly, before the second world war, Edward went off to England without even telling her. She was broken-hearted and each night she continued to light the candle and pray for him, hoping that some day he would return. The old lady got very sick and Edward was sent for, but by the time he returned his mother had died. From her death bed she had left a message with a neighbour to be given to her son. 'Tell Edward that I will leave a candle in the window of heaven for him.'

It takes little imagination to know her message - tell him that I will still care for him, tell him that I will always be close to him – to be his guide, his protector, his light.

As you listen today, you may feel very much alone and broken because your loved one has been taken from you and that part of your life is gone. It is at a time like this that we must deepen our trust. Our dead can still touch us in a very real way, if we open our hearts in deep faith to the Lord and to them.

Let us find comfort in the scriptures, which constantly remind us that, because of the resurrection of the Lord, we should have hope. 'In death life is changed not taken away,' or again, 'Do not let your heart be troubled, trust in God and trust in me.' Be guided by St Paul who said, 'Do not grieve like people who have no hope.' Have faith, have trust, be full of hope because, if your loved one could speak to you at this moment, he or she would say, 'Be at peace, for I have lit a candle in the window of heaven for you to guide you each day.'

41. I appreciate that friend

I heard a story some time ago about a dinner dance that was supposed to have taken place in heaven and a great night was had by all. All the different virtues went and really enjoyed themselves. Humility was there sitting at the bottom of the table looking very happy. Charity was cutting the meat and giving out the meat and potatoes in abundance – nobody was rationed. Patience was there waiting quite contented in absolutely no rush to get his dinner. He was prepared to wait. Faith and Hope were sitting together chatting about the fact that they were losing influence in the world below.

At the height of the meal, Charity noticed that two of the virtues were not speaking to one another. They seemed strangers. Charity was surprised because he had put them together on purpose, presuming they would be good friends. He came down to the two of them and, when he realised that they did not know each other, he introduced them. 'Kindness, I want you to meet Gratitude.' Both of the virtues were very surprised to find out who the other was. Kindness said to Gratitude, 'We are supposed to be always together,. Where one of us is the other should be also. Isn't it a great pity that we never met before?'

A spoilt child seldom says thanks. A solid, balanced child, who had to work for what he or she has got, will always be grateful. In the gospels, we are told of the ten lepers who received a great gift of healing from God. Nine of them quickly forgot the one who healed them. They are too spoilt and selfish to take time to say thanks. The one who is grateful, the one who returns to say thanks, is the one who should have been least likely to do so, the foreigner. If we really take time to look at our lives, the majority of us will have to admit that we have received so many blessings from God that we take for granted.

42. They say one good turn deserves another

One day some years, ago Fr Murphy was passing by a prison when a man stopped him, looking for a lift. 'Could I please have a lift to the next town, father?' 'I would be delighted,' he said, 'Get in. I will be glad of the company.' On their way out of the city, the man told Fr Pat that he had just got out of prison after serving a sentence of two years for pick-pocketing. Fr Pat became completely engrossed in the conversation as the man told him all about life in prison, so much so that he ran a red light on a very busy intersection. Seconds later, he could hear the siren and he knew he was the victim, so he pulled over. Out came the notebook and all the details were taken and the guard reminded him that he would be hearing further. Fr Pat could not be sure which he dreaded most – the embarrassment of facing his parishioners or the teasing he would get from his fellow priests.

They continued to chat but Fr Pat had more on his mind at this stage. At last they came to the little town where the ex-prisoner was to get out. Fr Pat stopped the car and gave him a friendly goodbye. Then, as the ex-pickpocket was leaving, he said, 'Thanks for the lift, father. One good turn deserves another, here's the traffic officer's note book.'

43. We must send the furniture ahead of us

A very wealthy society lady died and went to heaven. As she looked about, she noticed that her maid, who had died some time before her, was living in a very beautiful mansion, while she herself was assigned to a rather insignificant house. Immediately she complained to St Peter. 'Don't you know who I am? I am so-and-so, and yet I find that my maid has much more splendid accomodation than I have. What is the meaning of this?' St Peter replied, 'I am sorry you are disappointed, but you see, we can only build out of what you send up here, and we did the best we could for you out of what you sent to us while you were on earth.'

Maybe all of us, as we listen to that simple story, might reflect and ask ourselves how much have we sent ahead that could be used as building material. To put it very plainly, God can only reward us for what we do unselfishly for him or for others.

44. I love you that much

One day, while on visitation in my last parish, a mother told me of a little game that began between herself and her six-year-old son. Now and then she would ask him, 'How much do you love me?' and he would shrug his shoulders, walk back and forth a little bit, and then stand in front of her with his two hands about six inches apart and say 'That much.' Then, on a day that she would have brought him to the beach or off to town in the car, she would again ask him the famous question, 'How much do you love me?' and, again, with the shrug of the shoulders, he would stand in front of her with his hands about twelve inches apart and say, 'That much.' On some special occasion, such as his birthday or at Christmas, after she had given him his present, she would again ask, 'How much do you love me now?' and then, without a moment's hesitation, he would stretch his arms apart until they were almost leaving their sockets and say, 'That much.'

One day as he did this, she suddenly realised that this is how Christ hung on the cross. 'Ever since that day,' she said, 'when I look at the cross, I can see his outstretched arms saying to me, "I love you that much. I love you more than any human being can imagine."'

I am reminded of the great truth of Scripture that we can often let in one ear and out the other: Greater love than this can no one have, than to lay down his life for his friend.

45. Drawing wrong conclusions

There was an old woman who crossed the Brazilian frontier every day on a motor scooter, with a sack of sand behind her. The customs officer eventually became suspicious and inquired, 'What have you got in that sack?' 'Only sand, sir,' came the reply. The officer emptied the sack and, indeed, it contained nothing but sand. And so it went on for a month. One day, the officer said to the old woman, 'I won't arrest you or say anything to the police, but just tell me: are you smuggling or not?' 'Yes,' she answered truthfully. 'Well, what are you smuggling?' he pressed her. With a smile, she replied, 'Scooters.'

Yes, we can be so wrong in our judgements. I think it is fairly true to say that the more one knows about an issue the less one says. I have often sat in company where an issue came up in convers-ation. Some would rattle on and draw conclusions all over the place, knowing very little about the issue. At the same time, someone in the same company knowing the real situation, would just sit there in disgust. This is very sad when people are involved. It is sad to hear people criticised and condemned by others who only know few of the facts.

I wonder are you guilty. Have you the courage to reflect for a few moments and examine your conscience?

46. Maybe you are part of the problem

A young minister went to his first church with eager enthusiasm. To his disappointment, he found the services poorly attended and the spiritual life of the congregation at low ebb. He called from house to house seeking renewed interest, but several people said the Church was so dead that they did not care to attend. He discussed the situation with his parish committee and they agreed that the criticism was probably justified.

The pastor announced that, since the Church was considered dead, he would conduct its funeral the following Sunday. The church was crowded that day. In front of the pulpit was a coffin. The minister eulogised the deceased. He told how much the Church had accomplished in the past and expressed his sorrow over its untimely death. Then he invited the congregation to go forward and view the corpse. One by one, the people looked into the casket; each was amazed to see his own face reflected from a mirror in the bottom of the coffin. Many were shocked and indignant, but then each member began to realise that his or her own spiritual indifference was the reason the Church was dead.

47. Junk or treasure

One day a family on the street was spring cleaning. They had a trailer outside the front door into which all the junk was thrown. The next door neighbour noticed a cross that was thrown into the trailer so she went into the house and asked if she could have it. 'Of course you can,' she said, 'sure it is only a piece of junk.' The neighbour went back home very happy with herself since she thought it was a real treasure. She cleaned up the cross and was delighted with her find. That night, as all the family sat in front of the fire, her little son had the cross in his hands and was staring at it. The mother asked him why he was looking at it for so long, and he answered, 'Because it looks so much like Jesus.'

All of them looked at the same cross but all saw something different. One saw just junk, another a treasure, and a third saw Jesus. Jesus is fully present to all of us. but it is up to us to be aware of his presence.

48. I can hear a cricket somewhere

One day last summer two men were walking down a very busy street in Dublin. One of the men, Pat, had lived in Dublin for the last thirty-two years. His friend, Tom, had lived in the country all his life. As they walked down the street, Tom stopped and said, 'I can hear a cricket.' 'Get sense,' said Pat, 'how can you hear a cricket in the midst of all the noise?' 'Yes, I can,' he replied, and he turned into a side street to his left and walked straight to a window. There on the window-sill was the cricket that he had heard from a distance.

Pat looked at him in amazement and said, 'I can't believe that you could hear that cricket in the middle of the city noise. I have not heard the sound of a cricket in over thirty years.' 'You never heard it,' answered Tom, 'because your ears were not open and attuned to the voice of the cricket. My ears are always ready and open for every sound of the countryside.'

There is a message for us in this little story. Just as our ears must be open to the sounds of God's creatures before we will hear them, so also our ears must be open to Christ before he can touch and influence our lives. We go to Mass on a Sunday morning and what is our reaction to it? Does it mean very little to us and leave us cold, because our ears are not attuned and open to God's presence, or are we open and ready to hear God speaking to us, as Tom was open to the noise of the cricket?

We walk into a shop and two handicapped children run over to us to hug us. What is our reaction? Do we side-step the situation and get away as soon as possible to avoid embarrassment, or do we respond with love, because we know and sense that Christ shines through them? We are driving down a side road in our car and we see an old lady lying on the side of the road with a bag of shopping beside her. Do we coldly pass by saying we haven't time, or it is not our business, or do we stop and do all we can to help her, as Christ would?

We can only feel the presence of Christ if our hearts are open to his message and his presence in the people and the things about us.

49. Stop struggling and I can help you

A drowning ten-year-old boy was shouting and struggling in the water. His seventy-year-old granny stood on the side of the quay in agony, fright and grief. A tall young man walked up beside her and saw the young boy struggle for his life but made no attempt to help him, even though the old lady begged him again and again to do something for him. After some time, the boy began to get tired and the struggling lessened and he was getting much weaker. Then the man jumped into the water and brought the boy to safety. 'Why did you not save him sooner?' asked the now very grateful granny. 'I was losing hope, lady,' said the young man, 'I could not save him as long as he was struggling. He would have dragged both of us to the bottom. When he stopped struggling it was easy to save him.'

That is God's message to all of us in the gospels. We spend so much time rushing and racing and trying to solve all our problems, while the Lord asks us to stop struggling and to trust in him.

Do you remember the day Jesus went to visit Martha and Mary? Martha was rushing and racing about, trying to get an answer to everything, and Mary sat and spoke to Jesus. Jesus then spoke to Martha and said, 'Martha, Martha, you worry and fret about so many things, but so few are needed. In fact only one. Mary has chosen the better part.'

Or in Matthew's gospel, where Jesus tells us to trust in him completely if we want peace. 'That is why I am telling you not to worry about your life and what your are to eat, nor about your body and how you are to clothe it. Surely life means more than food and body more than clothing? Look at the birds in the sky. they do not sow or reap or gather into barns, yet your heavenly Father feeds them. Are you not worth much more than they are?'

Jesus does not want us just to do nothing, but not to be so concerned about having an answer to all our own problems, because he is there to help if we trust.

50. The local shopkeepers

I once knew a village where there were two shops and there was always a bit of rivalry between them. They would always try to be one up on each other, any chance they got. For years they were always niggling at each other even though there was never a very serious row. In the early 1970's, a big business family set up a supermarket in the middle of the village and, of course, this put great pressure on both shops. Within a very short time, the two of them, who used to be in opposition, became the best of friends, scheming with each other about how they were going to handle this common enemy – the supermarket.

As we look at the history of peoples of different faiths and religions, they often act like the two shopkeepers – suspicious of each other, half trusting each other and keeping a check in case they were giving too much on any issue. All religions should, in fact, be acting like the two shopkeepers who had to fight for each other against the big supermarket that could destroy them. The common enemy of all religions, and all people of goodwill, is evil and materialism, and we should be striving together for the good of all.

51. Always give your best

Once there was a rich man who wanted to do good. One day he noticed the miserable conditions in which a poor carpenter lived. The rich man called the carpenter in and commissioned him to build a beautiful house. 'I want this to be an ideal cottage. Use only the best materials, employ only the best workmen, and spare no expense.' He said that he was going on a journey and that he hoped the house would be finished when he returned.

The carpenter saw this as his great opportunity. So, he skimped on materials, hired inferior workers at low wages, covered their mistakes with paint, and cut corners wherever he could. When the rich man returned, the carpenter brought him the key and said, 'I have followed your instructions and built your house as you told me to.' 'I'm glad,' said the rich man, and, handing the keys back to the builder, he continued, 'Here are the keys. They are yours. I had you build this house for yourself. You and your family are to have it as my gift.'

In the years that followed, the carpenter never ceased to regret the way in which he cheated himself. 'Had I only known,' he would say to himself, 'that I was building this house for myself ... '

This is precisely the same message that God gives to all of us. He gives us so many years to live on earth and, during our time here, we are to build the quality of home we will have in heaven. Our building material is not blocks and wood but justice, peace, forgiveness, sensitivity, understanding, self-sacrifice and unselfish love.

I am sure you heard about the rich man who was very disappointed when he realised that his servant had a much more beautiful home than he had in heaven. However, the saint explained to him, 'You must understand that we only build your home up here with material you send ahead while you are still on earth.'

As you begin tomorrow, make sure your heavenly home will be as beautiful as you would want.

52. A new way of seeing

I was twenty years old at the time and it was my first year to do summer work as a student in America. Having worked hard on a building site all day, I was coming home on the subway about 6 p.m. when there was a complete blackout. I was terrified. The blackout only lasted eleven minutes but it seemed like three hours. People were crying, some were getting agitated with one another, and the smell of sweat and raw garlic did not add any flavour to the tense situation. Naturally, the conversation at work the next day was the blackout and one of the men working with me told me of something that happened to him during a blackout all over New York city in the forties. It was close to midnight and all went black. He was on the street with a crowd of strangers. When he mentioned the street he lived on, a man offered to lead him home. John accepted the offer and began to follow the man through the dark streets. 'Stay close to me and I promise to get you home,' the stranger said. They advanced slowly, cautiously and carefully. The stranger talked as he moved forward. He seemed sure of where he was going and showed little sign of fear. As they reached the end of the street John suddenly recognised where he was. It was only when they shook hands to say goodbye that John realised the man was blind. As they parted, the blind man said to him, 'When I went blind, eighteen years ago, I had to learn a new way of seeing.'

So often in the Gospel, Jesus accused the Jews and Pharisees of being physically able to see and yet being spiritually blind. Jesus constantly calls us to open our hearts to the new way of seeing. There are many forms of blindness:

Selfishness:	*This blinds us to the needs of others.*
Insensitivity:	*This blinds us to the hurt we are causing others.*
Snobbery:	*This blinds us to the equal dignity of others.*
Pride:	*This blinds us to our own faults.*
Prejudice:	*This blinds us to the truth.*
Hurry:	*This blinds us to the beauty of the world around us.*

Materialism:	*This blinds us to the spiritual values.*
Greed:	*This blinds us from being just to others.*
Apathy:	*This blinds us from recognising the risen Lord.*

Helen Keller, who was blind and deaf from nineteen months old wrote, 'The greatest calamity that can befall a person is not that he should be born blind, but that he should have eyes and yet fail to see.'

53. I witnessed a miracle

Let me tell you about a teenager whom we will call Tom. Getting on the train, he was very nervous and excited and you will soon see why. He sat opposite a middle-aged man that he had never met before, but he felt he should tell him his story.

He told him that he had just been released from reformatory school, where he had spent three years for robbery and other crimes. He realised how wrong he had been and he just wanted a second chance to go straight and to show that he was sorry. He felt so sorry for letting his family down and he hoped that they would forgive him. They had never visited him or written to him during the three years but he did realise that neither of his parents could write and that they were too poor to be able to come to the reformatory which was a long distance from their home. He wanted so much to be able to go home but he wanted to make sure that he was welcome. He wrote to his parents and asked them to give him a sign. His home was just beside the railway track and they had an old apple tree at the end of the garden. If they wanted him back, all they had to do was to put a white ribbon on the apple tree. If he was not welcome home, they were to put nothing on the tree and he would just pass on to some town where he knew no-one and no-one knew him.

As the train was close to home, he was so nervous that he could not look and he asked his new found friend to look for him. After a while, the man caught Tom by the shoulder with joy on his face and said, 'Just take a look!' Tom looked and saw the old apple tree and it was wearing not just one white ribbon but a whole host of ribbons. Tears ran down Tom's face and the bitterness and anger of the years washed away. The other man said later, 'I felt that I had witnessed a miracle.'

To be without Christ is to be homeless in the deepest sense of all. This day, the Lord awaits for you with a thousand white ribbons to welcome you back through the grace of the sacraments and through the peace that he alone can give.

54. Kindliness

Some of the old writers had an unusual ability to preach very effective sermons by means of very simple stories. Aesop, who wrote the story which I am about to tell, must certainly have had experience with the relative values of kindliness and severity in dealing with his fellow-man.

One day, he tells us, while the sun and the wind were having a discussion, the question arose as to which of the two was the stronger. The wind maintained he was much more powerful and effective than the sun. As the sun would by no means admit this, it was decided to hold a contest to determine the stronger. Called in to assist them and to be the judge in the contest was Lady Moon. She decided that a traveller upon earth was to be the object of the experiment. Whichever could force him to remove his cloak from his shoulders would be judged the stronger of the two. The wind made the first effort. As the traveller walked along, feeling the steady pressure of the wind blowing upon him, he wrapped his cloak the more securely around him and plodded on. The stronger the wind blew, the more closely did the traveller draw his cloak about him. Fiercer and ever fiercer grew the blasts of the wind, till it was, at last, blowing a mighty gale. Yet the traveller clung to his cloak.

At last, when the time limit set by the Lady Moon came, the wind ceased its efforts and the traveller still had his cloak.

Then the sun took its turn. As it shone down upon the traveller, he began to feel its effects. First, he loosened his cloak somewhat, but, as the sun rose higher and higher in the sky, the heat became so unbearable that, within a few minutes, the traveller removed his cloak, and so the sun won the contest.

We shall all achieve our objective with other people by warmth, kindness and gentleness, not by coldness, roughness, aggressiveness or force.

55. Don't miss your chance

Illustration: A glass full of sand
According to an old legend, when the wise men were following the Star of Bethlehem, they came to the house of a certain lady. They said to her, 'Come with us, we have seen his Star in the East and we are going to worship him.' 'Oh!' she said, 'I would love to go. I heard that he would be coming one day and I have been looking forward to it. But I can't go just now. I am very busy and I have to set my house in order. But later, as soon as I am ready, I will catch up to you and find him.'

But when her work was done, the wise men were out of sight, the star shone no more in the heavens and she never saw Jesus.

Just a story, but let's apply it to ourselves. Every Christmas is such a busy time for most of us, we have so many things to do. If we reflect back over the last few days, how much of this time did we actually give to God? You need not answer me, but answer it for yourself.

Please let me show you. I have here a glass, packed with sand. If someone came along and said to you, 'I will pour fifty valuable gold coins over your glass and any coins that stay in the glass you can keep them.' As you see, all the coins fall over the sides of the glass. Common sense would soon take over and you would throw the worthless sand away, so that you could catch your valuable coins.

Why not do the same for Jesus? Why not spend much less time at all the useless fussing about we do over Christmas and give more time to let the love, the spirit and the faith of Jesus seep into your bones?

56. Please God, help mam to start the car

How do you face life? Are you an optimist who wakes up in the morning and says, 'Good morning, God,' or a pessimist who is much more likely to say, 'Good God, it's morning.'

We are all familiar with the prayer of asking God for something. Little five-year-old Jimmy was travelling with his mother when the car broke down. Mum opened the bonnet, not knowing one end from the other, and tried to fix it. At one stage, she came back into the car and heard Jimmy praying, with his hands joined and his eyes closed. 'Please God, help mam to start this car and, if you can't come, please send my dad.'

But how often do we reflect on the numerous blessings God has given us in life, and stop and say 'Thanks'? It all depends on the way we look at life. Phillip Neri once said, 'I cried because I had no shoes until I saw someone without any feet.'

I once read about a well-known runner who was training for a very important race. He tells his story:

'One week before the race, I went out to the track for a run and sprained my ankle. I sat on the track, very sorry for myself, knowing that I would miss the race. I drove back home across the city that night, still angry. I had to stop at a pedestrian crossing where a young man, badly crippled, began to drag himself across the street. He seemed so slow and I was getting so annoyed as I waited, that he should hold me up. When he passed, I raced on until I stopped outside my own door and then I began to think. Here I am with many trophies and successes, angry because I am missing one race, and I passed a young man of my own age on the street who would give so much to be able to walk.'

Maybe the next time we feel hard done by, or that things are not going our way, we should reflect on the millions of people throughout the world who are much worse off than we are, and who would give so much to share some of our blessings. If we take more time to reflect on all that we have in life, we will not forget to turn to God and say thanks.

57. Let him touch you

Some time ago, I spoke to a man who was very depressed and had attempted suicide. I asked him, 'why did you do it?' He looked at me angrily and said, 'That's a silly question, father. I've made every possible mistake in life that you could make. I've ruined myself and my family. I've committed every possible sin in the book. I've no reason left to live. I don't want to go on.' I spent an hour with him, trying to say what I am now going to try and say in ninety seconds.

It is sad that so many of us do not experience the depth and breath of God's great mercy and love. Think of St Peter, who was chosen to be the leader of the Apostles. Christ had warned him of the danger and yet he denied him three times ... 'I don't even know the man you speak of.' Christ must have been very hurt and yet he looked on Peter with eyes of understanding and love.

Think of Judas, who sold his friend for thirty pieces of silver. When Judas entered the garden and betrayed him, Jesus still called him 'friend.' 'My friend, do what you are here for.' Even Judas would have been forgiven if he had turned to his saviour for healing and love.

Then we have the two examples on the cross, when Christ was at his weakest. If Jesus was ever to show hardness or lack of forgiveness, it would have been then. A thief had the neck to ask, 'Jesus,' he said, 'remember me when you come into your kingdom.' 'Indeed I promise you,' Jesus replied, 'today you will be with me in paradise.'

To the crowds whom he had loved and cared for, and who were now jeering at him and shouting for his death, he gave forgiveness. He raised his eyes to heaven and said, 'Father, forgive them for they know not what they do.'

That is the same merciful Christ that you and I will meet. A God of mercy, understanding, forgiveness and love.

58. How do you really feel?

I was returning home, having given a retreat up the country, when I passed this beautiful house by the side of the road. I love new houses so I stopped the car, got out and sat on the boot and admired with envy. A lady came up behind me and said, 'Hello, do you like my house?' and she brought me in to show me around. It contained every modern convenience possible – as they would say, 'not a penny spared.'

During our conversation, I realised that this beautiful house was only part of the picture. Her husband had died four years earlier, just after they had finished their dream house. He left her well off and secure in the material things of life, but it all meant so little. She experienced a loneliness inside that ate her asunder. Each morning she woke up in her house, full of the latest modcons, but yet so empty. She would exchange it all for a single room bed-sitter if she had the one she loved to share it with.

Loneliness is one of the great sicknesses of modern society. There is the loneliness of the widow or widower who, for the first few months after their partner's death, receive such great attention, but then, as life goes on, they can so often be left alone to battle with their pain or loss. There is the loneliness of the thirty-year-old who would give so much to be a good wife and mother, but the opportunity never came her way, or the country twenty-year-old in a Dublin bed-sitter, who does not find it easy to mix. Then there is the loneliness of the old person, whether living alone, in hospital or in a nursing home, whose greatest need is not the food that comes to the bedside, but the sound of a human voice that cares for them.

We, as Christian people, are called to be the hand of Christ, to bring comfort to those who are sick, to give time to those who are lonely.

59. Poor Marilda

Have you heard about the beautiful teenage girl called Marilda? Each day, she used to play with her friends in the fields overlooking the sea. One day, this very bad witch came along, kidnapped her and brought her away to an old castle. The first thing the witch set out to do was to persuade Marilda, by every means possible, that she was very ugly and horrible. The witch used to have many young men coming to her for advice each day and, if Marilda knew she was beautiful, she would begin to talk to them and, in the end, fall in love with one of them.

In time, the witch was successful, because each occasion a young man appeared Marilda would rush to her room and stay there. She continued to believe that she was ugly as the witch continued to tell her so. Then one day, as Marilda was combing her hair in her room, she noticed a young man peeping through the curtains. As they stared at one another for a few moments she noticed his eyes so full of love and tenderness. He did not think she was ugly; it was obvious to her that he thought she was very beautiful. She leaped through the window and off they went and lived happily ever after.

That's the way our movies used to end but they have changed, and so has our society. Our great challenge as caring Christian people today is to give people hope – to help people to believe in themselves – to help them to believe that they are precious in the eyes of God. Too often we are seen as a nation of knockers. We pull one another down rather than building each other up with confidence and encouragement. We are so quick with a word of criticism but so slow with a word of praise.

60. Keep your eyes on the ball

For most of us, the majority of things that happened in our childhood have gone back into our subconscious, but for some reason there are certain incidents that we never forget. I remember when I was very young I was sitting in the kitchen one day with my father, who was reading the paper. I said to him, 'I am bored, Dad. I have nothing to do.' 'I will give you something to do,' said my Father, 'and if you are able to do it right, I will give you half a crown.' He tore up one of the pages of the paper in about forty pieces and asked me to put it together. I remember starting to work on the floor with enthusiasm, thinking that this was going to be easy. However, the harder I worked the more frustrated I got and, after about an hour, I gave in. Then my father turned over all the pieces and only then did I discover that on the other side of the page was the face of a man which, of course, was so easy to put together. When I stuck all those pieces together the other side had to be correct as well.

When we look at life, with all its problems, we may get frustrated, hurt and depressed when we cannot solve them on our own. So let each one of us turn all our worries over to a loving Christ, just as we turn over the page of a paper, and our problems will not seem near so difficult. Jesus tells us in St Matthew's gospel, 'That is why I am telling you not to worry about your life and what you are to eat, not about your body and how you are to clothe it. Surely life means more than food and the body more than clothing.' Hand whatever worry you have today over to Christ and it will not seem so difficult.

61. Love can change anything

One of the most Christian families I have ever met is a family I visit each time I go to the United States. A family of eight - big business people with a great sense of justice, full of generosity, love, kindness, sensitivity and prayerfulness. It is a joy to share the love and friendship of their home.

But there was one exception to all of this. Paul was a drunkard and heavy into drugs. He had served three periods in jail for stealing, drug-pushing and beating up a bar-man. Each time I went to visit them, his mother would always have the same request, 'Please pray for Paul and talk to him.' But I knew that nothing I ever said to Paul made the slightest difference, because he felt he was in the gutter and he had not the strength to rise above it.

Three years ago, I went back to Florida to give missions. Having finished a mission, I went to visit my friends, expecting the same story: 'Please pray for Paul.' But no ... Paul was the first person I met, his hair cut, freshly shaven and a new suit. He introduced me to his plump little lady friend from New York. Both of them were madly in love and preparing for marriage. Later on he said to me, 'I thought I was nothing and nobody. I never realised that anyone would love me enough to want to marry me. Her great love for me has given me a meaning to my life I never had before.'

As I listened to him I thought Christ loves us a thousand times more than any human being is capable of loving and, if we could only be aware of his love, we would have the courage and strength to achieve anything:

> *to rise above all depression,*
> *to control any sinful habit,*
> *to become alive with a living faith,*
> *to be capable of all forgiveness,*
> *to reach out a hand of friendship to all people,*
> *to love those we find it hard to love,*
> *to forgive those we find it hard to forgive.*
> *The love of God for you and me today is more powerful than we can ever even imagine.*

62. Cool it! Have patience!

A priest was called to speak to an elderly man who was begging. In the course of the conversation, the priest discovered that the man had been neglecting his spiritual duties for more than a year. The old man seemed to be so indifferent towards God and the Church that the priest lost his temper completely and told him he was good for nothing, a worthless Catholic and, in the end, he showed the beggar the door.

That night, the priest dreamed that Almighty God was speaking to him concerning this same old man, 'I have put up with that old man for nearly seventy years,' said God, 'And you could not put up with him for even a few minutes.'

A simple legend with a strong message. Where is our patience tested? How patient are we with some old person who tells the same story a hundred times, or has habits that we object to? How patient are we with the difficult person at work? How patient are we with members of our family who do not live up to our expectations? How patient are we with the beggar on the road, who has many hurts that we are unaware of? How aware are we of how patient God is with us?

63. The answer is at the centre

The concert had been a great success and the auditorium had been packed with people. Next morning, four ladies came in to sweep it out. They started to work in the back four corners and intended to sweep down until they met in the centre. They started to shout messages at one another, without great success since they were so far apart. 'Come over here,' one said, 'and talk.' 'I will not,' replied the second, 'you may come over here,' and so the argument started, with the four of them shouting at the tops of their voices. One of them made the suggestion that they should meet in the centre of the auditorium and chat, so they all agreed. As they sat and chatted, they could have a good laugh at their foolishness in shouting across at each other when the answer was so simple.

The very same is true of life. We waste so much time, energy and frustration, concerned about our differences and, as the saying goes, 'making mountains out of molehills.' How often does our pride, our ambition, stop us from letting go and reaching the real truth, and to say, ' I am sorry,' where necessary?

Whether we speak of the community, of marriage or the family or neighbourhood, or place of work or country, the problem is often similar. Jealousy, pride, bitterness, misunderstanding and hatred can cause great hurt and pain. However, the answer to most of our differences is also the same. Just as the four ladies walked to the centre of the auditorium to meet, all of us in life must also walk to the centre, to Christ. For where there is bitterness and hatred, Christ cannot be present, where there is fighting, Christ cannot be present.

Jesus sent his apostles out to unite all people. Before he sent them, he showed them his wounded hands and feet to let them know that he was sending them out not as imperial conquerors, but as lambs among wolves ... to conquer by love and truth rather than by power and slickness. Jesus said, 'I came not to be served but to serve.' He washed the apostles feet as a sign to them. We must copy his attitude of humble service if we are to reach unity and peace.

64. He does answer, you know

How many times have you heard people say, 'God never answers my prayers.' Yet, the contrary is true. God always answers our prayers but not always in the way we expect. Perhaps one of the best examples is the one found in the story told concerning Augustine and his mother Monica.

At one period of his life, Augustine was far from being a saint. In fact he was living a very immoral life and, because of this, he was breaking his mother's heart. One day, Augustine came to his mother with the news that he was going to go to Italy. At that time, Italy was not noted for its sanctity. Monica was saddened and thought that Italy would finish off her son's faith. So she prayed to God and asked him, 'Please do not let my son go to Italy.' Augustine went to Italy, so Monica must have thought that God was not listening to her prayer.

But when Augustine got to Italy, he met St Ambrose and, through his meeting with him, was converted and became a great saint.

To all intents and purposes, God had refused Monica's prayer. Yet, in reality, he had answered it. All Monica wanted was her son's conversion and she thought Italy was the worst place in the world for this. But God knew differently - he knew perfectly well that Italy was the very place where his conversion would come about.

As we pray, we should not just pray for specific requests but rather, pray that God's will be done, since he knows what will ultimately be the best for us.

65. You must turn the latch

Most of us have seen the painting of Christ knocking on the door of a house, with the words below the picture: 'Behold I stand at the door and knock.' But there is another story behind the painting of that picture. When the artist had finished the painting, he took his little son into the studio.

'Sonny,' he said, 'Your daddy has just painted this new picture. Do you like it?' The little fellow examined it seriously for a few moments. 'Oh yes,' the boy spoke up, 'it's nice. But you've made a mistake, Daddy. You've forgotten something.' 'I've made a mistake – forgotten something?' 'Well,' replied his son triumphantly, 'you forgot to put a latch on the door and the man can't come in.' His father smiled and said, 'No sonny, your daddy didn't make a mistake. There is a latch on the door - but it's on the inside.'

Unless we, personally, open the door of our hearts to Christ, he will be forced forever to stand on the outside. The latch is in our hands.

We can close Christ out of our lives if we wish, or we can open our hearts and make him welcome. In other words we need not be surprised if Christ means nothing to us because this will probably be the case unless we want Christ to be part of our lives.

66. Blessed Virgin Mary

There are many beautiful legends told about Our Lady. There is one lovely one about a happening during her flight into Egypt.

As Mary hurried along with the little Lord Jesus in her arms and Joseph by her side, she came to a very large ploughed field in which a poor man was sowing the seed. Herod's soldiers were not far behind and there was no place to hide. As the sower looked up, Our Lady greeted him with the words, 'God keep you, good sower. Today you are sowing wheat, to-morrow you shall reap it.' With that, she took a few grains of wheat from him and cast them into the ground. Immediately, the seed took root and grew up at once, thick and high, and the Holy Family went into the wheat field to hide. Shortly afterwards, the soldiers came along and began to interrogate the poor old man who was still spell-bound at the miracle that he had just witnessed.
'Did you see a man, woman and a child pass by?' they asked him.
'I did,' he answered.
'When?' shouted one of Herod's officers.
'When the wheat was being sown,' he answered.
'The man is a fool,' retorted the officer, 'That was six months ago.'

67. Just reach out and touch him

The Holy Family were on their way to Egypt and the journey was very long and difficult. One evening, Our Lady could not travel any further as she was tired. She asked Joseph if he would go to one of the houses and ask if they could possibly stay the night. He was very lucky as the first house he went to made them very welcome. They entered the little house and found it occupied by a widowed mother and her fourteen-year-old daughter, who was paralysed in both arms.

After the evening meal was over, Our Lady did what any good mother would do. She firstly fed her baby, then began to sing him to sleep. Seated opposite Mary in the little room was the paralysed girl who never took her eyes of admiration off the baby Jesus.

'Would you like to nurse my baby?' asked Our Lady.
'I would love to,' said the girl, 'If only you would put him in my lap for a short while I would be happy.'
'Well, you just take him in your arms and nurse him as I am doing,' said the Mother of God.
'But Lady, I can't. I am paralysed and cannot move my arms.'
'Go on,' insisted Our Lady, 'Take him in your arms.'
At this stage the girl was in floods of tears as she tried to explain to Our Lady that she was not able to move.
'Do as I tell you,' said the Blessed Virgin, 'Reach out and take him in your arms.'
At that, the girl made an effort to move and suddenly the miracle happened – her arms moved and she was free. That was the reward God gave the little family for sheltering his Son and his Mother.

We also might remember, from this simple legend, that as long as we reach out for Jesus, God will give us the power, courage and strength that we might have considered impossible.

68. Gossip

A lady once went to confession to St Phillip Neri and confessed that she had been gossiping about others. As a penance, St Phillip told her to go out and buy an unplucked fowl in the market place and, during her walk back, she was to pull the feathers out one by one and scatter them along the way. Then she was to return to him and he would tell her what to do next. It seemed a strange penance, but she went off to the market place and did exactly what she was told, no doubt feeling a little foolish.

On her return, St Phillip praised her for her obedience. He said, 'Now to complete your penance you must go back and pick up all the feathers.' 'But father,' the lady exclaimed, 'You know that is impossible. The wind blew them away and I could never hope to capture them now.' 'Quite true,' the saint replied. 'Neither can you recall the damaging words about your neighbours which by this time have passed from one person to another.'

We also must be careful of what we say about our neighbour so as not to hurt them in any way. One great rule of thumb to live by is never to say anything about your neighbour that you would not like said about yourself.

69. Don't run away – face it

During the First World War, a certain pilot with his observer had gone out with their squadron and, while over the German lines, they became involved in a dogfight. The young pilot came out of the dogfight very much the worse for wear. The accompanying planes were nowhere to be seen. He and his observer were alone. A burst of machine gun fire had ripped the left wing of the plane wide open, the engine was missing badly on two cylinders, and they had used up all their ammunition. Slowly but surely, they were making their way toward their own lines when, coming toward them, at the same height as themselves, they spotted a formation of enemy planes, six in all. That was quite a handicap considering the state of their plane. The pilot spoke to his observer. 'What are we going to do now? Try to climb above them or go down and take a chance by 'hedge hopping' back home?' 'Do neither,' was the observer's reply. 'Well, what do you expect me to do when we come up to them? Blow 'em a few kisses as we pass?' Unperturbed, the observer remarked, 'Wait till you get to within about three hundred yards and then fly straight through them.' The pilot thought his observer had gone mad, but recalling how, through following the observer's advice on several occasions before, he had come safely through, he did as he was bid. Whether it was that the totally unexpected manoeuvre completely bewildered the oncoming enemy, or whether they too were out of ammunition, we'll never know. All we do know is that, as he raced for the leading machine of the enemy formation, the others opened up leaving a wide gap through which he dived, leaving his enemies behind him.

When difficulties, troubles and handicaps face you, fly straight through them. Then your difficulties will be where they ought to be – behind you.

70. Give it your best shot

The time was now. Jesus decided he was ready to choose his twelve apostles. Just advertising in the newspapers didn't seem thorough enough. So Jesus decided to hold an Olympics from which the twelve would be chosen. The people came from all over. The competition was fierce. Jesus had to judge all the events.

First came the prayer event. People had practised, and it showed in the speed with which they could recite the words. Some articulated the words with utmost precision. Some used big impressive words. Still others expressed lofty ideas. But when it came time for a winner to be selected, Jesus chose none. There didn't seem to be any heart in their prayers. They were just words.

Second came the worship event. These contestants too had done their homework. Some wore beautiful garments. Some used lots of incense. Some emphasised music. Other incorporated gestures. But again, when it was selection time, there was no winner. There didn't seem to be any heart in worship. It was too showy.

Third came the teaching event. This was a prepared group. Some came with elaborate posters. Some came with long, well-ordered talks. Some came with video-cassette recorders. Others came with their small groups to demonstrate 'process'. Again, no winners. There was no heart in their teaching. The methods seemed more important.

So the Olympics ended. No winners, no apostles. Exhausted after this long exasperating ordeal, Jesus went down to the lake to cool off and relax. Then the miracle happened. He saw people fishing. Now there were some people who put their hearts into what they did. So he chose them.

Jesus does not judge us by our abilities but by our availability.

71. Bad language

The teacher asked the girls in her class to write a composition of not more than two hundred words on 'Our new car'. When she examined the essays she found one which went as follows: 'Last week my daddy bought a new motorcar and took all of us for a drive. But when we were out in the middle of the country, he drove into a wall. We were four miles from the nearest telephone and the other one hundred and fifty-seven words were what daddy said on the way to the telephone but I do not think I should write them down.'

72. Message of peace

'Dear Friend, I sit here on the bank of a river and, though I cannot see clearly the other bank, I know you are there and I wonder who you are. You, too, long to cross the river so that we can get to know each other – share ideas and, best of all, greet each other as friends. But how to cross, that is the problem, as it is no ordinary river. Years of hatred, violence and war have polluted the waters and no one yet has managed to cross by struggling against the flow. If, then, we cannot cross through the river, let us build a bridge over it. One that will be high and strong, that will carry us safely over the troubled waters. We already have the building material. Make its foundations of kindness and brotherly love, the walls of trust and faith. No bridge was ever built from one bank, so let us both set to and begin at once. One day we shall meet in the middle.'

That is the message, pass it on and put it into practice.
Cardinal Cushing is credited with the following recipe for renewal:
    If all the sleeping folks will wake up,
    And all the lukewarm folks will fire up,
    And all the dishonest folks will confess up,
    And all the disgruntled folks will sweeten up,
    And all the discouraged folks will cheer up,
    And all the depressed folks will look up,
    And all the estranged folks will make up,
    And all the gossipers will shut up,
    And all the dry bones will shake up,
    And all the true soldiers will stand up,
    And all the Church members will pray up,
    Then you can have the world's greatest renewal.

73. It isn't the Church – it's you

If you want to have the kind of Church
Like the kind of a Church you like,
You needn't slip your clothes in a grip
And start on a long, long hike.
You'll only find what you left behind,
For there's nothing really new.
It's a knock at yourself when you knock your church;
It isn't the Church – it's you.

When everything seems to be going wrong,
And trouble seems everywhere brewing;
When prayer meeting, Young Peoples meeting, and all,
Seem simmering slowly - stewing,
Just take a look at yourself and say,
'What's the use of being blue?'
Are you doing your bit to make things hit?
It isn't the Church – it's you.

It's really strange sometimes, don't you know,
That things go as well as they do,
When we think of the little - the very small mite -
We add to the work of the few.
We sit, and stand round, and complain of what's done,
And we do very little but fuss.
Are we sharing our share of the burdens to bear?
It isn't the church – it's us.

So, if you want to have the kind of a Church
Like the kind of a Church you like,
Put off your guile, and put on your best smile,
And hike, my brother, just hike,
To the work of saving a few.
It isn't the Church that is wrong, my boy;
It isn't the Church – it's you.
Author Unknown

74. No excuse Sunday

To make it possible for everyone to attend church next Sunday, we are going to make it very special.

A cot will be placed in the Sanctuary
for those who say, 'Sunday is my only day to sleep.'

Eye drops will be available for those
with tired eyes from watching TV too late Saturday night.

We will have steel helmets for those
who say, 'The roof would cave in if I came to church.'

Blankets will be furnished for those who think
the church is too cold, and fans for those who say it is too hot.

We will have hearing aids for those
who say the Pastor speaks too softly,
and cotton for those who say he speaks too loudly.

Score cards for listening hypocrites present.

One hundred TV dinners for those who
can't go to church and cook dinner also.

A selection of trees and grasses for those
who like to see God in nature.

A putting green near the altar for those
who say, 'Sunday is my only day for golf.'

The Sanctuary will be decorated with both Christmas poinsettias and Easter lilies for those who have never seen the church without them.

Author unknown
(Taken from the 'Kitchen Klatter' *Magazine, Sept. '76.)*

75. Ten most wanted individuals

1. The person who has a ready smile and a pat on the back for others.

2. The person who can see his or her faults before he sees the faults of others.

3. The person who gives his or her money, time or talents without thought of others.

4. The person who gives himself or herself totally unto a project, and then gives the credit for its success to his or her helpers.

5. The person who is willing to say, 'I was wrong, I am sorry.'

6. The person who will look at temptation squarely and say 'No.'

7. The person who puts God's business above any other business.

8. The person who brings his or her children to Mass instead of sending them.

9. The person who tries to be the right example to every individual, rather than talk about it.

10. The person who has a passion to help rather than a passion to be helped.

76. The world is mine

Today upon a bus, I saw a lovely maid
with golden hair;
I envied her - she seemed so gay - and
wished I were as fair.
When suddenly she rose to leave, I saw
her hobble down the aisle;
She had one foot and wore a crutch, but
as she passed, a smile.
Oh, God, forgive me when I whine;
I have two feet - the world is mine!

And then I stopped to buy some sweets.
the lad that sold them had such charm,
I talked with him - he said to me,
'It's nice to talk with folks like you.
You see', he said, 'I'm blind.'
Oh, God, forgive me when I whine;
I have two eyes – the world is mine!

Then, walking down the street, I saw
a child with eyes of blue.
He stood and watched the others play;
It seemed he knew not what to do.
I stopped for a moment, then I said,
'Why don't you join the others, dear?'
He looked ahead without a word,
and then I knew he could not hear.
Oh, God, forgive me when I whine;
I have two ears - the world is mine!

With feet to take me where I'd go,
With eyes to see the sunset's glow,
With ears to hear what I would know,
Oh, God, forgive me when I whine;
I'm blessed, indeed! The world is mine. *(Anon)*

77. Everyone is lovable

Last summer, I performed a marriage ceremony for two friends of mine. At some stage during the wedding preparation, I asked Margaret what attracted her to Tom. 'In fact,' she said, ' at first I didn't like him at all. I thought he was pompous and starchy.' 'What changed your mind?' I asked. 'It's funny,' she said, 'but some of his friends told me he was crazy about me and, even without realising it, I began to be attracted to him. I saw so many good points that I never saw before. Maybe now I just wanted to see them.'

Almost all people are lovable if you want to love them. It depends very much on the attitude of mind we set out with. Like Margaret, we can see someone's failings and dwell on them but, like Margaret, hopefully, we can also love each person we come into contact with and see so many good points that we will be able to laugh at their failings.

St John's gospel reminds us:
    Our love is not to be just words or mere talk
    but something real and active.
    Only by this can we be certain
    that we are children of the truth.

78. Finish the story for me, please ...

One day mammy fish and baby fish were swimming in the ocean. Mammy fish said to baby fish, 'The ocean is a great blessing for us fish, because we can swim where we like and enjoy its magic.' Baby fish just shrugged its shoulders and was not the slightest bit impressed. It turned to its mother and said, 'So what! No big deal! I don't need this ocean of yours.' Mammy fish was very upset, and decided to teach her baby Joey a lesson.

One very warm afternoon, as both of them swam by the water's edge, mammy fish, with a flick of her tail, threw baby fish out on to the bank and left him there in the heat of the sun for half an hour. Then she pulled her baby back in, and he was exhausted by the heat of the sun. Baby Joey turned to his mother and said, 'I'm sorry for being so foolish, mam. You have to be without something before you appreciate it. From now on, I will take time to think and to appreciate my blessings.'

And then there was Mrs Murphy, who was praying in the church when her sixteen-year-old son came in to ask her what was keeping her. She told him that she was talking to God, and young Tom gave a cynical laugh and said, 'Mother, God means nothing to me. I don't need God. I can be happy without praying to anyone. I can make it on my own ...'

How would you finish the story?
Could Mrs Murphy learn anything from Mrs Fish?
Could Tom learn anything from Baby Fish?

79. Crocodiles are seldom friendly

The crocodile was hunting an easy catch one morning when she got tangled up in a net. She struggled back and forth for a long time to set herself free, but the more she struggled the tighter the strong net stopped her from moving. She lay on the ground exhausted, until a little boy came along. 'Little boy,' said the crocodile, 'Please set me free.' 'No,' answered the little boy, 'My daddy always told us to be very careful of crocodiles. You could kill us!' 'Oh, no!' said the crocodile, I love little boys, and I was only out to get some food for my own little ones.'

After much persuasion, the little boy started to untangle the net from the head of the crocodile. As soon as her head was free, the crocodile grabbed the little boy in her big jaws. The boy screamed and said, 'That is very unfair! I helped you to get free and now you are going to eat me!' 'I have nothing against you. I just want meat, and now that I have you, who cares about what is fair? That's the way life is!' 'Oh no!' said the boy, 'Let us at least ask someone else!'

The crocodile agreed. A few minutes later a bird landed on a tree nearby and, as soon as the boy saw the bird, he told it the whole story, expecting that the bird would take his side. But the bird shook its head and said, 'Sorry, little boy, but the crocodile is right. That is the way life is. Last year I spent weeks building a nest up in a tree to hatch out my little ones. I had my chicks and loved them very much. Each day I would bring them food, and I made sure that they were never hungry. Then, one day as I came back with the food, I saw a big snake crawling into the nest and eating all my little ones. There was nothing I could do to save them. Yes, the crocodile is right.'

The boy asked the crocodile for one more chance, and she agreed. An old donkey came along and the boy told him his story. The donkey looked very sad and said to the boy, 'I worked hard all my life for those who owned me, but as soon as I was too old to work, they kicked me out to fend for myself or die. I am afraid, little boy, that I have to admit that the crocodile is right. That is the way life is.'

'Please give me just one more chance,' pleaded the boy, and the crocodile agreed. A rabbit came running by and, once again, the boy gave him the story. The rabbit sat up on his back legs and said, 'Well, let's discuss this in a mature, sensible way, to see who is right. But, please Mrs Crocodile, leave the little boy out of your mouth as we do so.' The crocodile agreed, presuming that she could kill the boy anytime she wanted to. But, as soon as the rabbit distracted the crocodile, he said to the boy, 'Run!' and he ran over to the rabbit. 'Don't your people like crocodile meat? The crocodile is still partly tangled in the net, so run home and bring back your people and kill it!'

The boy ran home and collected some of the townspeople who came back to kill the crocodile. The boy's pet dog ran back with them, but as soon as he saw the rabbit, he killed it before the boy could stop him. The boy looked down at the rabbit and said, 'Yes, the crocodile is right. That is the way life is.'

On a more serious level, the life we live and experience is full of contradictions that we will never explain. Life is like a jigsaw puzzle that we try to put together, but with only some of the parts. There is no way of explaining the hunger, the torture, the evil, the suffering and the destruction of this world. Life is, and will always be, a mystery. We so often feel that evil is slicker and cuter than truth.

But one thing is certain: If we trust in God with all our hearts, God will give us the strength and courage to overcome all suffering and evil, and to experience a peace that God alone can give. God will give us healing in the way that God knows best.

SOME PROP HOMILIES

80. God is here

Ilustration: A portable radio

Do you see anything floating around in the air? Except for a few specks of dust, I don't. It looks to me like there is really nothing much at all in the air around us.

But that's not true! This portable radio will prove that there's more in the air than we can see. When I turn it on like this and turn the tuning dial, what happens? You hear a radio programme. Where did it come from? The radio's antenna pulled in the radio waves that are found right around it, right around us. Around us right now are the radio waves this radio is picking up. We don't see them, hear them, taste them, or feel them but they are there nevertheless.

The Bible says that God is spirit. One of the things about something that is spirit is that you can't see it! Like the radio waves, God is all round us right this moment even though we can't see him. Just as we need a radio to pick up radio waves so that we might hear them, so we need to use something that can help us feel that God is right with us. It's not any kind of an instrument. It's an attitude. It's called faith. The way you and I feel God's presence in our lives is by faith - believing that he is here with us even though we don't see him. God does not make himself magically appear so that people have to believe in him. He wants people like you and me to believe in him because we want to.

If we want to feel God close by, we must always believe he is there. We must love him, depend on him, try to please him as he watches us, and talk to him often. Then he will become more and more real to us.

Yes, there are radio waves in the air even though we can't see them. With the help of a radio we know they are there. And yes, God is right here with us now even though we can't see him. With the help of faith we can know he is here.

81. Unique and useful

Illustration: various tools such as a hammer, a screwdriver, a saw.
Look at the different tools I brought with me today. Here's a hammer, used to pound nails. This is a screwdriver, used for turning screws into wood or metal. This saw cuts wood.

Do you think it would work to use a screwdriver to pound nails, a saw to tighten screws, or a hammer to saw wood? Of course not! Each tool is designed to do one job but not the other. Does that mean the hammer isn't as good a tool, because it can't cut wood like the saw? Does it mean that a screwdriver is a better tool, simply because it can tighten a screw while a hammer or saw can't?

No, each tool is good in its own way and each tool has limits to what it can do well. Did you know that each one of us is a tool of God's?

He has made us with different gifts and abilities. Some of you may be good in music. Others can do well in sports. Still others are good in art or perhaps maths.

Each of us needs to remember not to do two things when it comes to talents and abilities:

First, don't be jealous of someone else, simply because he or she is better than you in something. You have your own talents and abilities. You may not always know what they are, but you have them.

Second, don't be proud that you can do some things better than other people. Remember that they will be better than you in some other way.

You may wonder if you can do anything at all. The answer is yes. Ask God to help you see what you are good at doing. Yes, everyone is unique with different interests and abilities. The important point we all need to remember is that no one is better than anyone else, we're just different!

82. The power of words

Illustration: A tube of toothpaste and a plate
I need a volunteer to do two things. First, take this tube of toothpaste and squeeze quite a large quantity out onto this plate. That's good. Now I want you to put the toothpaste back into the tube! What seems to be the problem? Can't you stuff it back in? Well, I know I've asked you to do the impossible. Once toothpaste is out of the tube you can't put it back.

Words are much like this toothpaste. Once we let them out of our mouths we really can't take them back. This means we should be careful of the words we let out of our mouths. For instance, some of the things we say about a person may not be true. Some of the words we say, when we are angry, aren't very nice and we don't really mean what we say. It's at times like this that we ask the person we have hurt to forgive us. But even if the person forgives us, he or she will have a hard time forgetting what we said. There is nothing you or I can do to completely take back something terrible we have said. It's like too much toothpaste being squeezed from the tube!

Being able to say words and communicate thoughts and ideas is a marvellous gift from God. Let's not misuse this wonderful ability by speaking words that hurt people. Ask Jesus to help you control your tongue. Ask him to help you say only the things you should say.

Remember, a word is a lot like toothpaste – once you let it out, you can't take it back.

83. The black spot

Illustration: A white cloth with a black spot in the centre of it
Even as you relax and listen, you will immediately notice something about this white cloth that I hold up in front of you. Your eyes will focus on the black spot. No matter how often you look away, each time you look back, the black spot is only a small section of this cloth ... most of it is a lovely white.

It is the same with life. Firstly, as we look on the lives of other people, we can be so quick to draw conclusions ... so quick to presume. I would now like you to think of some person or group of people that you dislike ... and then I ask you to reflect on why you dislike them. Most likely, you dislike them because of one or two incidents in the past that you did not like or that hurt you deeply. We can so easily forget all the love in the other person, all the goodness in his or her life. God calls us to stop looking at the black spot in the lives of others and instead to look at the large part of their life which, like this cloth, is white with goodness and love.

How often do we hear about husbands and wives who live in silence, tension and hurt for so long because of something that has been said or done? Maybe your hurt is understandable and honest discussion and apologies are necessary. But please do not become so preoccupied with anything that you are blinded from seeing everything else. The same can be said of conflicts between families or neighbours. So often we find people living with so much hate in their hearts, and passing it on from one generation to the next, because of some incident or black spot that has been blown out of all proportion. Search for the goodness that exists in the life of others, just as Christ searches for the goodness in your life.

Secondly, so often we meet people who only see the black spot in their own lives. The good Christian who lives in constant guilt because of some mistake or sin or their past. To those I say, please stop looking at the black spot in your own life. God sees all your efforts and your love.

84. The mirror and the pane of glass

I have here in front of me two pieces of glass - but both of them serve a very different purpose. If I look through this piece of glass, I can see everyone through it, but if I look at this piece of glass, I can only see myself - since it is a mirror.

It is the same with life. The person who helps others, just to get attention or to be admired or praised, is like the person who looks into the looking glass and sees only him or herself. We can spent so much of our time doing things for people when, in fact, our real reason for helping is a selfish one, wondering how it 'will reflect on us'. For example, the person who makes sure to sit on the right committee; the person who makes sure to be seen in the right circles, or the person who is more conscious of his or her popularity vote than the love of God that they pass on to another person.

Jesus went hard on the hypocrites and, remember, he knows exactly what we are thinking. In St Matthew's gospel, chapter 6, he warns us, 'Be careful not to parade your good deeds before men to attract their notice; by doing this you will lose all reward from your Father in heaven. So when you give alms, do not have it trumpeted before you: this is what the hypocrites do in the synagogues and in the streets to win men's admiration. I tell you solemnly, they have had their reward.'

Instead, he tells us that our left hand must not know what our right hand is doing. This is a big challenge - to reach out to others in love, in understanding, in forgiveness, not expecting any reward whatever. In another place in Scripture he says, 'If you love those who love you, what reward do you expect, for even the pagans do that much, do they not? Love your enemy.'

If we take God's command to love seriously, it is very difficult and very challenging, because to love without expecting any response in return is God's first commandment.

'I believe that we are inclined to remember and reflect on a story, long after we would remember even the bones of a straight-forward sermon.' So says the author, Fr Frank Barron, in his introduction. Numerous surveys on the effectiveness of homilies would appear to back-up this view, and also the view that the best homilies are short and to the point.

In this collection, Frank Barron offers a range of short and simple stories, mainly from his own observation of the lives, attitudes and behaviour of ordinary people. A comprehensive thematic index is included for the convenienve of preachers and teachers who are faced with dealing with a particular theme or occasion. The collection is rounded off with five illustrated or prop homilies which Frank Barron has found helpful and effective.

Fr Frank Barron is a priest of the Diocese of Ferns. He spent the first seventeen years of his priesthood in the House of Missions, Enniscorthy, from where he gave missions in Ireland, England, Scotland and Wales. He also gave youth retreats, retreats for religious and days of recollection. He now works as a priest in the Ferns diocese and also gives missions in North America. He is the Ferns Diocesan Adviser to secondary schools and Invalid Chaplain to the Ferns Pilgrimage to Lourdes.